U0732294

丝路汉语系列教材

丛书顾问：西安市人民政府外事办公室

编委会

总主编：董洪杰

编　委：王　静　　薛亚军　　白晓莉　　刘　宁
　　　　段舟杨　　马　娜　　袁晚晴　　秦　岭
　　　　柴　闫　　邵　滨　　李　勇

The Silk Road Chinese Series of Textbooks

Consultant：Foreign Affairs Office of Xi'an Municipal People's Government

Editorial Board

Chief Editor：Dong Hongjie

Editors：Wang Jing　　　　Xue Yajun　　Bai Xiaoli　　　　Liu Ning
　　　　　Duan Zhouyang　Ma Na　　　Yuan Wanqing　Qin Ling
　　　　　Chai Yan　　　　Shao Bin　　Li Yong

丝路汉语系列教材

董洪杰　总主编

中国电影

马　娜　袁晚晴　编著

Chinese Films

暨南大学出版社
JINAN UNIVERSITY PRESS

中国·广州

图书在版编目（CIP）数据

中国电影 = Chinese Films / 马娜，袁晚晴编著. —广州：暨南大学出版社，2023.1
(2025.3 重印)
丝路汉语系列教材/董洪杰总主编
ISBN 978 - 7 - 5668 - 3286 - 3

Ⅰ. ①中…　Ⅱ. ①马…②袁…　Ⅲ. ①电影—中国—汉语—对外汉语教学—教材
Ⅳ. ①H195.4

中国版本图书馆 CIP 数据核字（2022）第 024765 号

中国电影
ZHONGGUO DIANYING
编著者：马　娜　袁晚晴
···

出 版 人：阳　翼
策划编辑：杜小陆　黄志波
责任编辑：黄志波
责任校对：刘舜怡　王燕丽
责任印制：周一丹　郑玉婷

出版发行：暨南大学出版社（511434）
电　　话：总编室（8620）31105261
　　　　　营销部（8620）37331682　37331689
传　　真：（8620）31105289（办公室）　37331684（营销部）
网　　址：http://www.jnupress.com
排　　版：广州良弓广告有限公司
印　　刷：广州方迪数字印刷有限公司
开　　本：787mm×1092mm　1/16
印　　张：13.5
字　　数：260 千
版　　次：2023 年 1 月第 1 版
印　　次：2025 年 3 月第 2 次
定　　价：79.80 元

（暨大版图书如有印装质量问题，请与出版社总编室联系调换）

总　序

　　国际中文教育经历了过去几十年的蓬勃发展，已经取得了骄人的成绩。其重要表现除学生数量的迅速增加之外，更有学生学习质量的提高，具体表现是学习需求在广度上不断延展，日趋多元化，在专业化方面也有追求精深的趋势。如何编写适用于不同专业领域、满足不同学习者语言和知识需求的教材，是国际中文教育面临的一大挑战。西安文理学院文学院的教师们在过去多年教学经验的基础上，于近期研发了针对不同专业学生需求的人文类分众化系列教材，以期能将语言学习和对专业领域知识的探索有机结合起来，在语言平台上作适当延展，以更好地满足不同学习者，特别是高年级学习者的多元化中文学习需要。

　　为了编写好这套针对留学生的专业化、分众化教材，丝路汉语系列教材编委会的教师们在对国内相关教材需求和发展现状进行调查的基础上，听取各方意见，结合各自专长，从中国文学、中国艺术、中国电影、旅游汉语、幼儿汉语、新时代商务汉语、汉字、书法等不同角度着眼，完成了这套汉语教材的编写。

　　这一系列教材的主要特点首先是主题多样化。因涉及不同学科门类，所以在编写体例上不追求整齐划一，但作为丝路汉语系列教材，在内容上均立足西安，辐射全国，兼具地域性和普遍性。其次，广泛吸收各领域最新的研究成果和相关教材的既有优长，通过"读一读"等补充材料使教材兼具科学性和典型性。再次，图文并茂、生动形象地解释和说明学生不熟悉的文化内容；叙述力求深入浅出，充分体现汉语和中国文化对外传播的新理念，具有较强的可读性和传播价值。最后，有些教材设计了实践部分，如让学生自己动手，制作与课文内容相关的艺术作品等；有些教材增加了"看一看"部分，有意识地将书本学习与参观古迹、博物馆等课外活动有机结合起来，以期调动学生的学习积极性，充分利用本地文化资源提高学生的感性认识。

简言之，丝路汉语系列教材在编写方面作出了一些新的尝试和有益的探索，值得业内同行关注。

梁　霞

2020 年底于圣路易斯

（梁霞，美国华盛顿大学东亚系教授、中文语言项目负责人，美国中文教师学会会长）

General Preface

International Chinese education has experienced vigorous development in the past few decades. It has achieved remarkable results, as seen by the rapid increase in students enrollment and their improved learning quality. The telling example is the continuous diversification of learning needs, and the tendency towards in-depth specialization. How to design textbooks for different professional fields and meeting diverse learners' language and knowledge needs is a significant challenge to international Chinese education. Based on years of teaching experience, the teachers from Xi'an University School of Literature have recently developed a series of textbooks tailored to meet the needs of students of different majors, especially the learning needs of advanced-level learners, in the hope of properly combining the learning of Chinese language with exploration of professional knowledge.

While editing the Silk Road Chinese series of textbooks, the Editorial Board members from different fields of humanities, familiarized with the current situations of Chinese teaching materials and fully considered the opinions of researchers, Chinese teachers and international students, designed a series of Chinese textbooks such as Chinese Literature, Chinese Art, Chinese Films, Chinese for Tourism, Chinese for Young Children, New Era Business Chinese, Chinese Character, Calligraphy, etc.

The first and principal feature of this series of textbooks is diversity of topics. Because it includes multiple disciplines, it does not pursue uniformity in the compilation style. As the Silk Road Chinese series of textbooks, the content is based in Xi'an, and integrates cultural topics across the country, covering both regional and national themes. Secondly, it draws extensively on the latest researches in various fields and existing related textbooks, providing readers with many supplementary reading materials like "have a read", so that the textbook can be made with scientific and typical. Thirdly, there are many pictures complementing texts, which helps to explain unfamiliar cultural concepts to students. This series introduces the Chinese language and culture to the outside world, in a format that both readable and conversational achieved. Finally, some textbooks are designed with practice sessions, allowing students to make artworks related to the text content, etc.; and some chapters include "take a look" parts, utilizing local cultural resources to integrate book learning with extracurricular activities such as museums visit and historic sightseeing. These activities will motivate students' enthusiasm to learn Chinese culture.

In short, the Silk Road Chinese series of textbooks have demonstrated new thoughts and methods of Chinese teaching. I am recommending this series to all the researchers, teachers and learners of Chinese language.

Liang Xia
December, 2020
From St. Louis

(Liang Xia, a professor at Department of East Asian Languages and Cultures, head of Chinese Language Program, Washington University, USA; president of Chinese Language Teachers Association, USA)

前　言

中国电影自 1905 年诞生以来，在国家文化建设与对外交流中发挥了重要的作用。近年来，中国电影的发展更是受到了全世界的瞩目。国家电影局的统计数据显示，2021 年及 2022 年，中国电影仅在中国内地的票房累计就分别达到 399.27 亿元人民币及 300.67 亿元人民币。中国已经成为历史上第一个电影票房超越美国好莱坞的国家，成为全球第一大票仓。

在中国电影如火如荼的发展历程中，有诸多优秀的电影作品和电影人给其他国家的观众带来了震撼和影响。电影作为国家形象的展示窗口，引领世界认识中国，了解中国社会，同时也通过讲述中国人的故事，让世界熟悉我们国家的历史文化和民俗风貌。而陕西西安作为中国电影进入新时期之后的重镇，孕育了以西安电影制片厂作品为代表的中国西部电影，为中国电影的发展贡献了大量经典电影作品，不仅将国际三大 A 类电影节的奖项悉数收入囊中，还让更多的国家和地区将目光投射到中国西部地区。在这样的背景下，开发一本立足陕西西安、面向留学生的中国电影教材，既顺应了教育部关于"新文科"建设和学科交叉融合的发展背景，又以电影的视角展示了中国及陕西西安悠久的历史文化特色与丰富的语言资源。

《中国电影》共分为"西部映像""都市百态""奇幻武侠"三个篇章，除了上编特别突出陕西西安的地域文化特征外，其他两个篇章分别选取世界电影发展中最受各国观众喜爱和关注的题材类型，生动呈现中国源远流长的历史文化和社会现代化的发展进程。内容上，本书以影片赏析的方式和简洁明了的语言介绍电影，辅以对汉语词语、语境的教学，以及对中国文化的全方位展示，使学习者通过电影轻松地掌握汉语知识，全景式了解中国社会文化。

全书将电影、语言、文化三者的学习融为一体，使学生在了解电影的同时，直观生动地掌握中国及陕西西安的社会生活和文化特征。尤其是在每一小节后的延伸阅读，开创性地将语言、地理、历史、民俗等内容与电影学习相结合，对学生的学习领域进行拓展，实现全方位、多层次的覆盖。

　　作为丝路汉语系列教材之一，《中国电影》以电影为纽带，以汉语学习和文化传播为目的，助力于国家形象塑造与文化输出，既是一本供对外汉语教学使用的中国电影教材，也可为学生学习汉语、了解中国社会文化生活提供帮助。

马　娜　袁晚晴

2023 年 1 月

Foreword

Since its birth in 1905, the Chinese films industry has played an important role in national cultural construction and foreign exchange. In recent years, the development of Chinese films has attracted international attention. In 2021 and 2022, the cumulative box office of Chinese films in Chinese Mainland alone still reached 39,927 billion yuan and 30,067 billion yuan, according to the statistics data released by the State Film Administration. It suggests that China has become the first country in history to overtake Hollywood in terms of the box office and has accumulated the most box office across the world.

With the development of Chinese films in full swing, many excellent films and filmmakers have brought entertainment and influence on audiences in other countries. As a window to display China, the film industry directs the world to understand her people and society. At the same time, it also tells the stories of Chinese people to familiarize the world with our country's history, culture and folk customs. Xi'an, Shaanxi Province, as an important city after Chinese films entered the new era, gave birth to Western Chinese films represented by the works of Xi'an Film Studio, and contributed to a large number of classic aiding the development of Chinese films. It not only received all the awards of the three international first class film festivals, provided opportunities for other countries to become interested in Western China. In this context, the development of a Chinese Film textbook for foreign students based on Xi'an, Shaanxi Province, not only follows the development supported by the Ministry of Education on the construction of "New Liberal Arts" and interdisciplinary integration, but also shows the long historical and cultural characteristics and rich language resources of China and Xi'an, Shaanxi Province, from the film's perspective.

Chinese Films is divided into three chapters: "Western Image", "Urban Forms" and "Martial Arts Fantasy". In addition to highlighting the regional cultural characteristics of Xi'an, Shaanxi Province, in the first part, the other two chapters respectively portray the theme types that are most loved and appreciated by audiences all over the world in the development of films, presenting China's long-standing history and culture, along with the development process of social modernization vividly. In terms of content, this book introduces the films in the way of film appreciation and concise language, supplemented by the teaching of Chinese words and context, as well as the all-round display of Chinese culture, so that the learners can easily master the Chinese language knowledge and have a panoramic understanding of Chinese society and culture through the films.

Throughout the book, the study of films, language and culture is integrated, allowing students to understand the films and intuitively and vividly grasp the social life and cultural characteristics of China and Xi'an, Shaanxi Province. In particular, the extended reading after each section creatively combines language, geography, history, folk customs and other content with film learning to expand students' learning fields and realize all-round and multi-level coverage.

As one of the Silk Road Chinese series of textbooks, *Chinese Films* employs films as the portal to disseminate Chinese learning and culture, thereby helping shape the national image and social paradigm. This publication is not only a Chinese film textbook for teaching Chinese as a foreign language, but also a tool to assist students in learning Chinese and understand China's social and cultural life.

Ma Na, Yuan Wanqing
January, 2023

目录

Contents

上 编

西部映像

Volume I

Western Image

　　西部电影是新时期以来中国电影发展史上重要的组成部分，它以中国西部地域特色、风土人情为背景，展现了人们生存困境与精神品质。

　　陕西西安是西部电影发展重镇，孕育了诸多影响中国电影的重量级作品，也培养了一批优秀的中国电影人。

　　《红高粱》《白鹿原》和《双旗镇刀客》三部作品在题材类型和艺术风格上各不相同，但都是代表中国文学和电影创作的经典之作。通过这三个单元的学习，可以使学生掌握中国西部电影的主要特征和发展概况。

Western films has played a critical role in the history of Chinese films development since modern times. This kind of films shows the difficulty in lives and the spiritual quality of characters against the background of regional characteristics and local customs in Western China.

Xi'an, Shaanxi Province, is a strategic city for the development of western films. It has bred many inspirational works affecting Chinese films and cultivated a number of superlative Chinese filmmakers.

The three works of *Red Sorghum*, *White Deer Plain* and *The Swordsman in Double Flag Town* are very different in subject, matter, type and artistic style, but they all represent the classics of Chinese literature and film creation. By studying these three units, students will be able to master the main features and development of Western Chinese films.

第一单元
红高粱

本单元重点

1.了解电影《红高粱》的艺术特色
2.了解张艺谋导演的艺术风格

本单元难点

1.了解红色在电影中的寓意
2.了解中国著名作家莫言的文学成就
3.分析电影的主题思想

Unit 1
Red Sorghum

📢 Key points

1.Learn about the artistic characteristics of *Red Sorghum*
2.Learn about the artistic style of director Zhang Yimou

📢 Difficult points

1.Know about the symbol of red in this film
2.Know about the literature achievements of famous
Chinese writer Mo Yan
3.Analyze the theme extolled in this film

《红高粱》：中华儿女的热血赞歌

Red Sorghum：The Warm-Blooded Hymn of the Chinese People

一、丝路放映厅 Silk Road screen hall

导演：张艺谋

编剧：莫言/陈剑雨/朱伟

主演：姜文/巩俐

类型：剧情/战争

制片国家/地区：中国内地

上映日期：1988－02（柏林国际电影节）

　　　　　1988－05－19（中国香港）

片长：91 分钟

英文名：*Red Sorghum*

改编自莫言的同名小说《红高粱》

Director：Zhang Yimou

Screenwriter：Mo Yan/Chen Jianyu/Zhu Wei

Starring：Jiang Wen/Gong Li

Type：Drama/War

Production country/region：Chinese mainland

Release date：February，1988（Berlin International Film Festival）

　　　　　　　May 19，1988（Hong Kong，China）

Length：91 minutes

English name：*Red Sorghum*

Adapted from Mo Yan's novel of the same name *Red Sorghum*

主要获奖 Major awards

第三十八届柏林国际电影节：金熊奖

第八届中国电影金鸡奖：最佳故事片、最佳摄影、最佳音乐、最佳录音、最佳导演、最佳男主角

第十一届大众电影百花奖：最佳故事片

The 38th Berlin International Film Festival：Golden Bear Award

The 8th Golden Rooster Award for Chinese Film：Best Feature Film，Best Photography，Best Music，Best Recording，Best Director and Best Actor

The 11th Hundred Flowers Award：Best Feature Film

剧情梗概 Plot synopsis

影片从"我"口中讲述"我奶奶"九儿和"我爷爷"余占鳌的故事。九儿（巩俐饰）19岁那年因十八里坡的李大头给了一头骡子作为彩礼出嫁，余占鳌（姜文饰）以轿夫的身份负责把轿子抬到十八里坡，路过高粱地里时被打劫。轿夫们把钱都交了出来，劫匪还强制要奶奶跟他走。余占鳌及轿夫们将劫匪失手打死，余占鳌与九儿两人一见钟情。不久李大头死了，九儿扛下了烧酒作坊。土匪三炮劫走了九儿，逼着坊里拿钱赎身，罗汉等人筹资换回了九儿。高粱酒里撒了一泡尿，没想到酒的味道格外好，九儿起名为十八里红。后来，日本人来青杀口修路，用武力逼着百姓踩平高粱，并且活剥了罗汉。九儿组织烧酒作坊众人开始了勇敢的对抗。九儿被日本人的机枪打死，愤怒的余占鳌决定和大伙与日军同归于尽。余占鳌和儿子站在九儿尸体旁，大声唱起了童谣："娘，娘，上西南，宽宽的大路，长长的宝船……"一段传奇落幕。

The story of this film is told by the narrator as "I"，about "my grandmother" Jiu'er，and "my grandfather" Yu Zhan'ao. Jiu'er（played by Gong Li）was married to Li Datou at the age of 19 years old，because Li Datou of Shibali slope paid a mule as bride price. Yu Zhan'ao（played by Jiang Wen）was responsible for carrying the sedan chair to Shibali slope as a chair carrier. But they were robbed when passing through the sorghum field. The sedan bearers had handed over all the money，but still the robbers forced grandmother to go with them. Yu Zhan'ao and the other sedan chair bearers killed the robbers by accident. Yu Zhan'ao and Jiu'er fell in love at first sight. Soon，Li Datou died and Jiu'er managed the brewery. The bandits Sanpao kidnapped Jiu'er forcing the brewery to give them the money to buy back her freedom. Luo Han and others raised money in exchange for Jiu'er. There was a bubble of urine in sorghum wine. Unexpectedly，the wine tasted particularly good. Jiu'er named it the Shibali red. Later，the Japanese came to Qingshakou to build roads and forced people to smooth sorghum. They stripped Luohan alive. Jiu'er organized the people of the brewery to begin a brave confrontation. Jiu'er was killed by the Japanese army's machine guns. Yu Zhan'ao became angry and decided to perish together with the Japanese army. Yu Zhan'ao and his son stood beside Jiu'er's body and sang a nursery rhyme loudly："Mum，mum，go to the southwest，through the wide roads，on the long treasure boats…" and the legend ended.

重要词汇 Important vocabularies

打劫	dǎjié	*vt.*	rob
一见钟情	yījiàn-zhōngqíng		fall in love at first sight
高粱	gāo·liang	*n.*	sorghum
赎身	shú//shēn	*v.*	buy back one's freedom
愤怒	fènnù	*adj.*	angry
童谣	tóngyáo	*n.*	nursery rhyme
传奇	chuánqí	*n.*	legend

例句 Example sentences

1. 昨天，路口的金店遭遇了打劫。

Yesterday，the gold shop at the intersection was robbed.

2. 一见钟情的剧情，常常出现在爱情电影里。

The plot of fall in love at first sight often appears in love films.

3. 高粱是酿酒的好材料。

Sorghum is a good material for brewing.

4. 赎身需要一笔不菲的费用。

It will cost a lot to buy back one's freedom.

5. 他不停地抱怨，她感到十分愤怒。

She is very angry about his endless complaints.

6. 每个国家和地区都有脍炙人口的童谣。

There are popular nursery rhymes in every country and region.

7. 他的丰功伟绩终将成为传奇。

His achievements will eventually become legend.

语言练习 Language practices

请为以下句子选择合适的词语进行填空。

Please fill in the blanks with the appropriate words for the following sentences.

1. 罗宾汉是英国历史中的（　　　　）人物。

Robin Hood is a（　　　　）character in British history.

2. 紧握的双手展现了他（　　　　）的情绪。

The clenched hands showed his（　　　　）mood.

3. 《小星星》是一首广为流传的（　　　　）。

Little Star is a popular（　　　　）.

4. 最近，警方破获了一起金店（　　　　）案。

Recently, the police cracked a gold shop（　　　　）case.

5. （　　　　）后，你就不再被束缚。

After（　　　　）, you will not be constrained.

6. 我和他（　　　　），浪漫极了。

I（　　　　）with him（　　　　）, which was so romantic.

7. 一望无际的（　　　　），象征着旺盛的生命。

The endless（　　　　）symbolizes vigorous life.

二、丝路大讲堂 Silk Road lecture hall

【导演特色】Featuring director

张艺谋，1950年4月2日出生于陕西西安，是中国第五代电影导演的领军人物之一，毕业于北京电影学院摄影系。他的电影主要改编自现实主义题材文学作品，且善于使用色彩语言，融入了鲜明的中国元素，在各类型影片中形成了独特的审美观念和中国式的创新。张艺谋的作品在屡获国际大奖的同时，具有不俗的票房号召力，兼具艺术和商业价值，真正做到了"雅俗共存"，使中国电影真正地走向了世界的舞台。

张艺谋的艺术成就颇丰，在陈凯歌导演的《黄土地》（1984年）一片中担任摄影师，以演员的身份主演了吴天明导演的《老井》（1986年），夺得"东京电影节最佳男演员"的称号，并担任 2008 年北京奥运会开幕式和闭幕式总导演。其代表作品有《菊豆》（1990 年）、《秋菊打官司》（1992 年）、《有话好好说》（1997 年）、《英雄》（2002 年）、《长城》（2016 年）、《影》（2018 年）等。

Zhang Yimou, born in Xi'an, Shaanxi Province, on April 2, 1950, is one of the leaders of China's fifth generation of film directors. He graduated from the Photography Department of Beijing Film Academy. His films are mainly adapted from realistic literary works and he is excel at using language of color. In various types of films, he has formed a unique aesthetic concept and Chinese-style innovation. While winning many international awards, Zhang Yimou's works not only have good box office appeal, but also have artistic and commercial value. They truly achieve the "coexistence of elegance and vulgarity" and truly bring Chinese films to the world stage.

Zhang Yimou has achieved great artistic success. He worked as a photographer in *Yellow Earth*（1984）, directed by Chen Kaige. He starred as an actor in *Old Well*（1986）, directed by Wu Tianming, and won the title of "best actor in Tokyo Film Festival". Then, he was appointed as the general director of the opening and closing ceremonies of the 2008 Beijing Olympic Games. His representative works include *Ju Dou*（1990）, *The Story of Qiu Ju*（1992）, *Keep Cool*（1997）, *Hero*（2002）, *The Great Wall*（2016）, *Shadow*（2018）, etc.

【红色的象征】 The symbol of red

影片《红高粱》的总基调为红色，张艺谋导演擅长运用色彩的"表意"作用。从人物到空间，都大面积运用红色，片中有红色的衣服、红色的高粱，还有红色的太阳和土壤，红色贯穿了影片的主色调和局部色调，在传达导演创作意图和构建美学风格的同时，给观众以强烈的视觉冲击。

红色在中国电影中有以下几种含义：

（1）代表喜庆： 传统的红色象征着喜庆、吉祥，在中国民间风俗中多用于喜事，逢年过节、新婚之喜都要装点红色，以求吉利。片中九儿出嫁，红鞭炮一响，九儿坐着红色的花轿，穿着红色的衣服与鞋子，这是中国民间婚庆的典型习俗。鲜红的轿子是喜庆的，九儿却要被迫嫁给五十多岁的李大头，此处是张艺谋对红色以喜衬悲的诠释。

（2）**代表热情与血性**：片中罗汉酿出的红色的高粱酒，还有田中浓密的红高粱、红色的土地象征中华儿女豪迈的姿态，是他们蓬勃的原始生命力的写照。红色为本片营造了炙热、疯狂的氛围，是中华儿女热血、勇敢的精神象征。

（3）**代表鲜血与暴力**：红色也是鲜血的颜色，给人以暴力、不安的躁动感。放在日本卡车上的血红色的牛皮，再到影片结尾九儿遭到日军杀害后，红色高粱酒的破碎，整个画面被异样的鲜红色笼罩。此处的红色有血腥暴力之意，也是对日军在战争中残忍行为的无声控诉。

The general tone of the film *Red Sorghum* is red. Director Zhang Yimou excels at using the "ideographic" function of color. From the characters to space, red is widely used. There are red clothes, red sorghum, red sun and soil in the film. Red runs through as the main color and local tone of the film, which not only conveys the director's creative intention and constructs the aesthetic style, but also gives the audience a strong visual impact.

Red has the following meanings in Chinese films:

（1）**Represents festivity**: the traditional red symbolizes festivity and auspiciousness. It is mostly used for festive events in Chinese folk customs. During New Year's Day or other festivals and wedding celebrations, it should be decorated with red in order to be lucky. In the film, Jiu'er gets married and the red firecracker rings. Jiu'er sits in a red sedan chair and wears red clothes and shoes, which is a typical custom of Chinese folk wedding. The bright red sedan chair is festive, but Jiu'er is forced to marry Li Datou, who is in his fifties. Here is Zhang Yimou's interpretation of red as joy against sorrow.

（2）**Represents enthusiasm and courage and uprightness**: the red sorghum wine brewed by Luo Han in the film, the thick red sorghum in the field and the red land symbolizes the heroic attitude of the Chinese people, which is a portrayal of their vigorous primitive vitality. Red creates a hot and crazy atmosphere for the film. It is the spiritual symbol of the blood and courage of the Chinese people.

（3）**Represents blood and violence**: red is also the color of blood, giving people a violent and restless feeling. The blood red cowhide on the Japanese truck, and then at the end of the film, after Jiu'er was killed by the Japanese army, the red sorghum wine was broken and the whole picture was shrouded in a strange bright red. The red here represents blood and violence and is also a silent protest against the cruel acts of the Japanese army in the war.

【民族音乐】 Folk music

片中音乐由著名作曲家赵季平创作，在环境音的基础上凸显了民族乐器的韵味，将唢呐、笙和鼓组合起来，构筑出具有交响乐独特性的音响造型，使影片充满浓厚的中国西北地域特色。颠轿时高亢明亮的唢呐声，加上西北嘹亮的民歌以及特有的男高音，将黄土高原的豪迈风情，以及人身上喷涌而出的原始生命力展示给观众。其中《酒神曲》《颠轿曲》等几首插曲也是广为流传。人声的演唱极具民族特色，粗犷有力，高亢的嗓音借鉴了陕西陕北地区民歌的表现方法，淳朴自然却不失美感。音乐是电影画面的补充，也是电影视听构成中重要的有机组成部分，能够起到塑造人物、深化主题的作用。片中的《妹妹曲》运用了山东地区戏曲和陕西秦腔的元素，高亢得接近嘶吼的男声演唱配上随风摇曳的高粱，展示了生命力的旺盛；《酒神曲》《颠轿曲》都富有阳刚之气，展示了西北男人的真性情，特别是《酒神曲》出现在抗日的背景下，表达了民众的抗日决心和视死如归的英雄气概。

The music in the film is created by the famous composer Zhao Jiping, which highlights the charm of Chinese national musical instruments on the basis of environmental sound. Suona, Sheng and drum are combined to build a unique sound shape with symphony, which make the film full of strong regional characteristics of Northwest China. The sonorous and bright suona sound, coupled with the loud folk songs in the northwest and the unique tenor, show the heroic style of the Loess Plateau and the original vitality gushing from people to the audience. Among them, several episodes such as "Dionysian Song" and "Sedan Chair Bumping Song" are also widely spread. The singing of human voice has great national characteristics, rough and powerful. The high-pitched voice draws lessons from the expression method of folk songs in Northern Shaanxi, which is simple, natural, but aesthetic. Music is not only the supplement of motion pictures, but also an important organic part of film audio-visual composition. It can shape characters and deepen themes. "Sister Theme Song in the film" uses the elements of Shandong Opera and Shaanxi Opera. The high-pitched male singing close to roaring, coupled with sorghum swaying with the wind, shows the exuberance of vitality. Both "Dionysian Song" and "Sedan Chair Bumping Song" are full of masculinity, which show the real personality of men in Northwest China. In particular, "Dionysian Song" appears in the background of anti-Japanese sentiment, expressing the people's determination to resist Japan and the heroic spirit of treating death as home.

【人物塑造】Characterization

九儿因家庭贫困，19 岁时被李大头以一头骡子的价格定亲。九儿是片中唯一的女性，她不同于中国封建社会中的传统女性，不甘于服从命运的安排，憎恨封建社会的伦理纲常对人性的束缚。她善良、单纯，却敢爱敢恨，勇于追求自己的爱情。面对外敌对中国的入侵，她用生命保卫了家园，举起反抗侵略者的大旗。余占鳌是典型的西北汉子，为了自己心爱的女子，敢于冲破封建礼教的束缚。他疾恶如仇，对于伤害心爱之人的人绝不姑息，血性方刚，敢于同外来势力作斗争。《红高粱》中的英雄都不是传统意义上的伟大人物，九儿和余占鳌张扬了普通人身上的个性，巧妙地将爱国主义和个人意志的抒发融合在一起。

Jiu'er was engaged to Li Datou at the age of 19 at the price of a mule because of the poverty of Jiu'er's family. Jiu'er is the only woman in the film. She is different from the traditional women in Chinese feudal society. She is unwilling to submit to the arrangement of fate and hates the shackles of human nature often imposed by the ethics of feudal society. She is kind and simple, but dares to love and hate and dares to pursue her own love. Facing the invasion of China by foreign enemies, she defends her home with her life and raises the banner of resistance against the invaders. Yu Zhan'ao is a typical northwest man. For the sake of his beloved woman, he dares to break through the shackles of feudal ethics. He has an abhorrence of sin. He does not tolerate that somebody would hurt his beloved. He is vigorous and brave, and dares to fight against foreign forces. The heroes in *Red Sorghum* are not great figures in the traditional sense. Jiu'er and Yu Zhan'ao expose the personality of ordinary people and skillfully integrate patriotism and the expression of personal will.

【张艺谋电影中的女性】Women in Zhang Yimou's films

《秋菊打官司》（1992 年）：电影中的女主人公秋菊生活在中国西北的一个农村，丈夫在与村长争执时被踢伤下体。面对村长的拒不道歉，秋菊走上了维权之路，怀着身孕的她从乡上告到县上，执意要"讨个说法"。本片的许多场景采用了"偷拍"的方式，呈现出了极强的纪实效果。本片获得了第 49 届威尼斯电影节金狮奖。

《一个都不能少》（1999 年）：14 岁的山村少女魏敏芝是本片的主角，她来到山里的小学当代课老师。她给校长承诺，班里孩子一个都不能少。一个 10 岁的孩子张慧科因为家庭贫困，不得不辍学去城里打工。面对陌生的城市，魏敏芝为了坚守"一个都不能少"的承诺独自上路了，经过一番磨难，最终借助媒体的力量找回了张慧科。

《我的父亲母亲》（1999 年）：村里的少女招娣爱上了村里新来的青年教师骆老师，在那个闭塞的年代，招娣不顾他人的眼光，大胆追求着自己的心上人。她给骆老师送饭，为了特意听到骆老师的琅琅读书声，挑水绕远路，每天都在骆老师回家的路上等着他。历经磨难，两个有情人终在一起，相爱相守四十年，成为流传的爱情佳话。

The Story of Qiu Ju（1992）：the heroine Qiu Ju lives in a rural area in Northwest China. Her husband got his private parts kicked and injured while arguing with the village head. Faced with the village head's refusal to apologize, Qiu Ju embarked on the road of safeguarding her husband's rights. She was pregnant and appealed to the county from the countryside and insisted on "asking for an explanation". Many scenes in this film adopt the way of "candid shooting", showing a strong documentary effect. The film won the Golden Lion Award of the 49th Venice Film Festival.

Not One Less（1999）：Wei Minzhi, a 14-year-old mountain village girl, is the protagonist of the film. She came to be a substitute teacher in a primary school in the mountains. She promised the headmaster that none of the children in the class can be less. Zhang Huike, a 10-year-old child, had to drop out of school to work in the city because of his poor family. In the face of a strange city, Wei Minzhi embarked on the road alone in order to adhere to the promise of "not one less". After some hardships, she finally recovered Zhang Huike with the help of the media.

The Road Home（1999）：Zhaodi, a young girl in the village, fell in love with Mr. Luo, a new young teacher in the village. In those closed years, Zhaodi ignored the eyes of others and boldly pursued her sweetheart. She sent meals to Mr. Luo. In order to specially hear Mr. Luo's reading voice, she carried water around the long way and waited for Mr. Luo's way home every day. After much suffering, the two lovers finally got together and remained true to each other for 40 years, which became a popular love story.

【高粱与十八里红】Sorghum and Shibali red

张艺谋在导演阐述里说道：《红高粱》通过人物个性的塑造来赞美生命，赞美生命那种喷涌不尽的勃勃生机，赞美生命的自由、舒展。《红高粱》中大片的高粱在银幕上翻飞流动，金色的阳光下，逆光拍摄狂舞的高粱分外耀眼。高粱代表的是中华民族旺盛的生命力，是在强权面前不愿屈服、自力更生的生命状态。高粱酿成的酒，余占鳌的"尿"居然成了十八里红的点睛之笔。这种设定强化了十八里红所象征的不拘一格的自由精神。众人在决定与日军拼死对抗前，敬酒神，一饮而尽，用手中的大刀冲向侵略者的机枪，用身躯担起守卫祖国的重任。敢爱敢恨的中华儿女，崇尚生命的力量，这也是张艺谋写出的生命赞歌。

Zhang Yimou said in the director's exposition：*Red Sorghum* praises life through the shaping of characters' personality，praises the endless vitality of life，and praises the freedom and stretch of life. In *Red Sorghum*，a large area of sorghum flies and flows on the screen. Under the golden sun，the sorghum dancing against the light is particularly dazzling. Sorghum represents the exuberant vitality of the Chinese nation. It is a state of life that is unwilling to yield and self-reliance in the face of power. The wine made from sorghum，Yu Zhan'ao's "urine" has actually become the finishing touch of Shibali red. This setting strengthens the spirit of freedom symbolized by the Shibali red. Before they decided to fight the Japanese army to the death，they toasted God，drank it all in one gulp，rushed at the aggressor's machine gun with their broadswords，and shouldered the heavy responsibility of guarding the motherland with their bodies. The Chinese people who dare to love and hate，advocate the power of life，which is also the hymn of life written by Zhang Yimou.

【其他版本】 Other versions

由张艺谋执导、莫言编剧的《红高粱》斩获国际大奖，成为中国电影走向世界的引路碑、第五代导演的经典之作。此后，莫言的《红高粱家族》被改编为其他艺术作品：

（1）豫剧《红高粱》：2012年参与文化部举办的全国优秀剧目展演获得相关奖项。

（2）评剧《红高粱》：2015年在天津评剧院首演。

（3）舞剧《红高粱》：2013年首演，青岛市歌舞剧院创作演出。舞剧版本基本保留了小说原著以及电影《红高粱》故事的主线情节，分为颠轿、野合、祭酒、丰收、屠杀、出殡六大章节，以芭蕾舞的形式再现了这个传奇故事。

（4）电视剧《红高粱》：2014年中国大陆首播，共六十集。电视剧版由郑晓龙执导，周迅饰演主人公"九儿"，更为详细地还原了原创剧本。

Directed by Zhang Yimou and written by Mo Yan，*Red Sorghum* won an international award and became a standard for Chinese films to the world and a classic of the fifth generation of directors. Since then，Mo Yan's *Red Sorghum Clan* has been adapted into other works of art：

（1）Henan opera *Red Sorghum*：participated in the national excellent play exhibition held by the Ministry of culture in 2012 and won relevant awards.

（2）Pingju opera *Red Sorghum*：premiered in Tianjin Pingju Opera Theater in 2015.

（3）Dance drama *Red Sorghum*：premiered in 2013，created and performed by Qingdao song and dance theater. The dance drama version basically retains the main plot of the original novel and the story of the film *Red Sorghum*. It is divided into six chapters：sedan chair bumping，field adultery，wine offering，harvest，slaughter and funeral，which reproduces this legendary story in the form of ballet.

（4）The TV series *Red Sorghum*：it was first broadcast in Chinese mainland in 2014，with a total of sixty episodes. Directed by Zheng Xiaolong，Zhou Xun plays the protagonist "Jiu'er"，the TV drama version restores the original script in more detail.

互动讨论 Interactive discussion

结合剧情和老师的讲解，试着回答以下问题。

Combining the plot with the teacher's explanation，try to answer the following questions.

1. 电影《红高粱》中讲故事的"我"是谁？

Who is the "I" telling the story in the film *Red Sorghum*?

2. 谈谈你对本片中红色的理解。

Talk about your understanding of red in this film.

3. 你还看过张艺谋的其他电影吗？是否喜欢？说说看。

Have you seen other films directed by Zhang Yimou? Did you like them? Give your opinions.

三、延伸阅读 Extended reading

1. 莫言 Mo Yan

莫言，原名管谟业，1955 年生于山东省高密市，毕业于北京师范大学，是中国当代著名作家，2011 年先后获得韩国万海文学奖、中国茅盾文学奖，2012 年摘得诺贝尔文学奖的金冠，成为首位获得该国际奖项的中国作家。

其创作风格以"大胆"著称，带有明显的先锋色彩，是"寻根文学"作家流派的代表人物之一。在对中国乡土的写作中，莫言融入了富有传奇色彩的自我创造，善用联想、梦境、幻觉等写作手法，写动物故事、鬼怪故事和人的传奇，形成了独特的魔幻现实主义的小说风格。除此之外，莫言的小说也充满了对本民族历史和现实的审视，具有强烈的反思精神和批评意识，其作品具有"世界文学"的品质。莫言的小说代表作品有《红高粱家族》《生死疲劳》《丰乳肥臀》《蛙》《檀香刑》《食草家族》等。

Mo Yan, formerly known as Guan Moye, was born in Gaomi County-level City, Shandong Province in 1955 and graduated from Beijing Normal University. He is a famous contemporary Chinese writer. In 2011, he successively won the South Korean Manhae Prize for Literature and the Chinese Mao Dun Literature Award. In 2012, he won the gold crown of the Nobel Literature Award, becoming the first Chinese writer to win this international award.

His creative style is famous for its "boldness" and has an obvious vanguard color. He is one of the representatives of the writer school of "root seeking literature". In the writing of Chinese countryside, it integrates legendary self-creation, makes good use of writing techniques such as association, dream and illusion, and writes animal stories, ghost stories and human legends, forming a unique magical realistic novel style. In addition, Mo Yan's novels are also full of examination of the national history and reality, with a strong spirit of reflection and criticism, and his works have the quality of "world literature". Representative works of Mo Yan's novels include *Red Sorghum Clan*, *Life and Death Are Wearing Me Out*, *Big Breasts and Wide Hips*, *Frog*, *Sandalwood Death* and *The Herbivorous Family*.

影视改编 Film and television adaptations

1. 电影《红高粱》（1988 年）改编自莫言的小说《红高粱家族》。

The film *Red Sorghum* (1988) is adapted from Mo Yan's novel *Red Sorghum Clan*.

2. 电影《暖》（2004 年）改编自小说《白狗秋千架》，由霍建起导演。

The film *Nuan* (2004) is adapted from the novel *White Dog Swing Fram*, directed by Huo Jianqi.

3. 电影《幸福时光》（2000 年），改编自小说《师傅越来越幽默》，由张艺谋导演。

The film *Happy Times* (2000) is adapted from the novel *Shifu, You'll Do Anything for a Laugh*, directed by Zhang Yimou.

4. 话剧《我们的荆轲》，是北京人艺 2011 年的大剧场剧目，由莫言任编剧、任鸣任导演。

The play *Our Jing Ke* is the Grand Theater play of Beijing People's art in 2011, written by Mo Yan and directed by Ren Ming.

5. 电影《太阳有耳》（1995 年）改编自小说《白棉花》，由严浩执导。

The film *The Sun Has Ears*（1995）is adapted from the novel *Cotton Fleece*, directed by Yan Hao.

2. 中国山东 Shandong，China

山东省，简称"鲁"，位于中国东部沿海，分别与河南、河北、安徽、江苏四省接壤，省会为济南市。全省陆域面积为 15.58 万平方千米。主要城市有济南市、青岛市、烟台市、菏泽市、济宁市、日照市等。

Shandong Province, referred to as "Lu" for short, is located on the eastern coast of China, bordering Henan, Hebei, Anhui and Jiangsu provinces respectively. The provincial capital is Jinan. The land area of the whole province is 155,800 square kilometers. The main cities are Jinan, Qingdao, Yantai, Heze, Jining, Rizhao, etc.

地理环境 Geographical environment

山东省位于黄河下游，地处温带季风性气候区，降水集中，光照充足，境内中部多山峦，"五岳"之首泰山屹立于中部，西北部、西南部地形平坦，易形成湖泊。

Shandong Province is located in the lower reaches of the Yellow River. It lies in the temperate monsoon climate area with concentrated precipitation and plentiful sunlight. There are many mountains in the middle of the territory. Mount Tai, the first of the "Five Sacred Mountains", stands in the middle. The terrain in the northwest and southwest is flat and easy to form lakes.

旅游资源 Tourist resources

山东省历史悠久，古有齐古都临淄，今有革命圣地台儿庄，山东共有 6 处国家 5A 级风景区、10 座历史文化名城，山东民风淳朴，"好客山东欢迎您"一度作为山东省的广告语。主要景点有青岛市的栈桥、崂山、八大关，济南市的趵突泉、千佛山，烟台市的蓬莱阁，"五岳"之一的泰山等。

Shandong Province has a long history. In ancient times, there was Linzi, the ancient capital of Qi, and now there is Tai'erzhuang, the holy land of revolution. Shandong has 6 national 5A scenic spots, 10 famous historical and cultural cities, simple folk customs. "Hospitable Shandong welcomes you" was once used as the slogan of Shandong Province. The main scenic spots include Zhanqiao, Laoshan and Badaguan in Qingdao, Baotu Spring and Qianfo Mountain in Jinan, Penglai Pavilion in Yantai, and Mount Tai, one of the "Five Sacred Mountains".

孔子 Confucius

孔子，名丘，字仲尼，是中国古代著名的思想家、教育家、政治家，儒家学派创始人，被世人尊称为"孔圣人"，由其弟子编撰他的言语而成的《论语》闻名于世，以孔子为代表的儒家思想是中国文化的根基，对全世界都产生了深远的影响。山东省的曲阜市是孔子的故乡。

Confucius, named Qiu and surnamed Zhongni, was a famous thinker, educator, politician and founder of Confucianism in ancient China. He's respected as "Confucius the sage" by the world. *The Analects of Confucius* compiled by his disciples is famous all over the world. Confucianism represented by Confucius is the foundation of Chinese culture and has a far-reaching impact on the whole world. Qufu City in Shandong Province is the hometown of Confucius.

鲁班 Lu Ban

鲁班，春秋时期鲁国人，是中国土木工匠的始祖，他的发明创造对中国的农业、建筑业都有影响。鲁班的发明创造有锯子、曲尺、伞、石磨等。中国建筑业联合会以鲁班为名设立了"建筑工程鲁班奖"，是中国建筑工程质量方面的最高荣誉。位于大雁塔旁的陕西省历史博物馆，以及位于西安市长安区的陕西师范大学新校区图书馆，都曾获得鲁班奖的表彰。

Lu Ban, a native of the state of Lu in the Spring and Autumn period, was the ancestor of

Chinese civil craftsmen. His inventions and creations had an impact on China's agriculture and construction industry. Lu Ban's inventions include the saw, ruler, umbrella, stone mill, etc. The China Construction Industry Federation has set up the "Construction Engineering Lu Ban Award" in the name of Lu Ban, which is the highest honor award of the China construction industry. The Shaanxi Provincial History Museum, which is next to the Wild Goose Pagoda and the library of the new campus of Shaanxi Normal University in Chang'an District of Xi'an, have both won the Lu Ban Award.

泰山 Mount Tai

泰山，素有"天下第一山"之称，国家 5A 级旅游景区，有着"盘古开天地"的美丽传说。泰山是古代皇帝祭祀神灵、封禅之宝地，主要景点有阴阳界、桃花峪、玉皇顶、傲徕峰等。

Mount Tai, known as "the first mountain in the world", is a national 5A tourist attraction with a beautiful legend of "Pangu opens the world". Mount Tai is a treasure place for ancient emperors to offer sacrifices to gods and worship deities. The main scenic spots include Yin and Yang Circles, Peach Blossom Valley, Jade Emperor Peak, Mount Aolai, etc.

胶州秧歌 Jiaozhou Yangko

胶州秧歌又称地秧歌、跑秧歌，是山东省的传统民俗舞蹈之一，是山东省三大秧歌之一。该舞种起源于清朝，至今已经有两百多年历史。胶州秧歌于 2006 年成功入选国家级非物质文化遗产名录。

Jiaozhou Yangko, also known as local Yangko and running Yangko, is one of the traditional folk dances in Shandong Province and one of the three major Yangko in Shandong Province. This dance originated in the Qing Dynasty and has a history of more than 200 years. Jiaozhou Yangko was successfully enrolled into the national intangible cultural heritage list in 2006.

渔民节 Fishermen's Day

山东胶州地区捕捞的节日，至今已有三百余年历史，通常是渔民为了祈福风调雨顺，祭拜东海龙王而举行的庆祝活动。近年来，每到渔民节，大量的游客前来观赏，热闹非凡，当地也推出了多种旅游项目，如贝壳节、渔家乐等。

The fishing festival in Jiaozhou, Shandong Province, has a history of more than 300 years. It is usually a celebration held by fishermen to pray for good weather and worship the Dragon King of the East Sea. In recent years, a large number of tourists have come to watch fishermen's day, which is very lively. A variety of local tourism projects have been launched, such as the shell festival, fisherman's fun, etc.

四、课后思考 After class thinking

1. 《红高粱》中最吸引你的中国民俗是什么？

What is the most attractive Chinese folk custom in *Red Sorghum* for you?

2. 你所在的国家有没有人得过诺贝尔文学奖？他们是谁？有哪些成就？

Has anyone in your country won the Nobel Prize for literature? Who are they? What are their achievements?

五、互动时间 Interaction time

观赏电影片段，学唱影片中的经典插曲《妹妹你大胆地往前走》。

Watch the movie clips and learn to sing the classic episode "Sister, You Go Ahead Boldly".

妹妹你大胆地往前走

作词：张艺谋

作曲：赵季平

妹妹你大胆地往前走呀

往前走　莫回呀头

通天的大路　九千九百

九千九百九呀

妹妹你大胆地往前走呀

往前走　莫回呀头

从此后

你搭起那红绣楼呀

抛洒着红绣球呀

正打中我的头呀

与你喝一壶呀

红红的高粱酒呀

红红的高粱酒呀嘿

Sister，You Go Ahead Boldly

Lyricist：Zhang Yimou

Composer：Zhao Jiping

Sister，you go ahead boldly

Go ahead and don't turn back

The road leading to heaven is 9,900

9,990

Sister，you go ahead boldly

Go ahead and don't turn back

Since then

You put up the red embellished building

Throwing red Hydrangea

It's hitting me on the head

Drink a pot with you

Red sorghum wine

Red sorghum wine hey

第二单元
白鹿原

本单元重点

1.了解电影《白鹿原》的艺术特色
2.了解陕西关中地区的概况

本单元难点

1.分析本片中的主要人物形象
2.了解《白鹿原》的时代背景

Unit 2
White Deer Plain

📢 Key points

1.Learn about the artistic characteristics of *White Deer Plain*
2.Learn about the basic facts of the area Guanzhong Shaanxi

📢 Difficult points

1.Analyze the protagonists portrayed in this film
2.Know about the time background set in *White Deer Plain*

《白鹿原》：黄土高原上的风土人情

White Deer Plain：Local Customs on the Loess Plateau

一、丝路放映厅 Silk Road screen hall

导演：王全安

编剧：王全安/陈忠实/芦苇

主演：张丰毅/段奕宏/吴刚/张雨绮

类型：剧情/历史

制片国家/地区：中国大陆

上映日期：2012－02－15（柏林国际电影节）

　　　　　2012－09－15（中国大陆）

片长：188分钟（柏林国际电影节）

　　　156分钟（中国大陆）

英文名：*White Deer Plain*

Director：Wang Quan'an

Screenwriter：Wang Quan'an/Chen Zhongshi/Lu Wei

Starring：Zhang Fengyi/Duan Yihong/Wu Gang/Zhang Yuqi

Type：Drama/History

Producer countries/regions：Chinese mainland

Release date：February 15，2012（Berlin International Film Festival）

　　　　　　　　September 15，2012（Chinese mainland）

Length：188 minutes（Berlin International Film Festival）

　　　　　156 minutes（Chinese mainland）

English name：*White Deer Plain*

主要获奖 Major awards

第六十二届柏林国际电影节：银熊奖、杰出艺术成就奖

卢茨·赖特迈尔第十三届华语电影传媒大奖

观众票选最受瞩目男演员：段奕宏

The 62nd Berlin International Film Festival：Silver Bear Award and Outstanding Artistic Achievement Award

Lutz Wright Meyer 13th Chinese Film Media Award

The most watched actor in the audience's vote：Duan Yihong

剧情概述 Plot synopsis

影片改编自陈忠实的同名小说《白鹿原》。小说中白、鹿两个家族世代居住在白鹿原上，乡约鹿子霖（吴刚饰）之子鹿兆鹏为追寻自由，离开家乡，投身于革命事业。白家长工鹿三（刘威饰）之子黑娃与地主家的三姨太田小娥（张雨绮饰）私通，两人逃回到白鹿原准备成亲，却被以族长白嘉轩为首的家族拒绝接纳，被迫搬到村外窑洞内栖身。加入共产党的鹿兆鹏回到家乡后，掀起了一场革命浪潮，黑娃受到启示，加入革命。革命失败后，两人被迫逃亡。鹿子霖趁机强占了独自留守在家的田小娥，并诱使田小娥与现任族长白嘉轩（张丰毅饰）之子白孝文（成泰燊饰）发生关系，以打击白家的威望。白嘉轩当众惩戒白孝文，并与其断绝父子关系，从而引发族内矛盾。白孝文将家产变卖给鹿子霖，后因为贫穷卖身当兵，留下已经怀孕的田小娥一人。一天夜里，鹿三来到窑洞，杀死了田小娥。成为土匪的黑娃回家后，发现田小娥已死，大闹白家，鹿三在羞愤中上吊自杀。随着日军的侵袭，白鹿原这片古老的土地又将面临翻天覆地的变化……

The film is adapted from Chen Zhongshi's novel of the same name *White Deer Plain*. In the novel, the Bai and Lu families have lived on the White Deer Plain for generations. Lu Zhaopeng, the son of village official Lu Zilin (played by Wu Gang), left his hometown to devote himself to the revolutionary cause in pursuit of freedom. Heiwa, the son of a longtime worker of Bai's—Lu San (played by Liu Wei), had an affair with Tian Xiao'e (played by Zhang Yuqi), the third concubine of the landlord. They fled back to the White Deer Plain to get married, but they were rejected by the family headed by Bai Jiaxuan, the head of the clan, and were forced to move to the kiln cave outside the village.　After Lu Zhaopeng, who joined the Communist Party, returned to his hometown, there was a wave of revolution. Heiwa was inspired to join the revolution.　After the failure of the revolution, the two were forced to flee.　Lu Zilin took the opportunity to seize Tian Xiao'e who stays at home alone, and seduced Tian Xiao'e to have an affair with Bai Xiaowen (played by Cheng Taishen), the son of the current patriarch Bai Jiaxuan (played by Zhang Fengyi), in order to reduce the prestige of the Bai's.　Bai Jiaxuan punished Bai Xiaowen in public and cut off the relationship between father and son, which led to contradictions within the family.　Bai Xiaowen sold his family property to Lu Zilin.　Later, he became a soldier because of poverty, leaving Tian Xiao'e alone, who was pregnant.　One night, Lu San came to the cave and killed Tian Xiao'e. Heiwa, who had become a bandit, went home and found Tian Xiao'e dead.　He made a scene at the Bai's.　Lu San hanged himself in shame and anger.　With the invasion of the Japanese army, the ancient land of White Deer Plain would face earth shaking changes.

重要词汇 Important vocabularies

自由	zìyóu	*n.*	freedom
革命	gémìng	*n.*	revolution
成亲	chéng//qīn	*v.*	get married
逃亡	táowáng	*v.*	flee
怀孕	huái//yùn	*v.*	pregnant
土匪	tǔfěi	*n.*	bandit
古老	gǔlǎo	*adj.*	ancient

例句 Example sentences

1. 笼中的鸟儿失去了自由。

The birds in the cage had lost their freedom.

2. 辛亥革命的成功标志着封建制度的灭亡。

The success of the revolution of 1911 marked the demise of the feudal system.

3. 在中国古代，成亲的流程相当烦琐。

In ancient China, the process of getting married was quite arduous.

4. 四处逃亡的生活，让他心有余悸。

The life of flee around made him feel a lingering fear.

5. 女性怀孕生孩子是人类伟大的举动。

It is a great human achievement for women to pregnant and have children.

6. 山里的土匪已经被剿灭了。

The bandits in the mountains have been eliminated.

7. 世界各地都流传着古老的传说。

There are ancient legends all over the world.

语言练习 Language practices

请为以下句子选择合适的词语进行填空。

Please fill in the blanks with the appropriate words for the following sentences.

1. （   ）的东方有一条龙，它的名字叫中国。

There is a dragon in the （   ） east whose name is China.

2. 烧杀抢掠的（   ）毁掉了整个村庄。

Burning, killing and looting, the （   ） destroyed the whole village.

3. （   ）会让女性产生诸多身体和心理上的变化。

（   ） will cause women to have many physical and psychological changes.

4. 今天是我们（   ）的大喜之日。

Today is our great day of （   ）.

5. （   ）的号角已经吹响。

The horn of （   ） has sounded.

6. 任何人都不能非法限制他人的人身（   ）。

No one can illegally restrict the personal （   ） of others.

7. 在（   ）的过程中，他们又杀害了几个无辜的人。

In the process of （   ）, they killed several innocent people.

二、丝路大讲堂 Silk Road screen hall

【导演特色】Featuring director

王全安，陕西延安人，中国第六代电影导演代表人物之一。童年时有学习绘画的经历，20 世纪 80 年代考进北京电影学院表演系，先后出演了多部影片。1999 年，执导个人首部电影《月蚀》，荣获第 22 届莫斯科国际电影节国际评委大奖。其作品《图雅的婚事》（2006 年）荣获第 57 届柏林国际电影节金熊奖。王全安善于将戏剧性融入现实主义题材的作品中，使其作品既有人文关怀，关注底层生活，特别是关注中国女性的生存境况，也有强烈的戏剧冲突和叙事张力。王全安在西安电影制片厂工作的经历，使他拍摄了许多中国西部题材的作品，例如蒙古族题材的《图雅的婚事》、以西安城市为背景的《纺织姑娘》（2010 年）以及史诗作品《白鹿原》（2012 年），展现出十分鲜明的地域风情。

Wang Quan'an, born in Yan'an City, Shaanxi Province, is one of the representatives of China's sixth generation film directors. He learned painting in his childhood. In the 1980s, he was admitted to the performance Department of Beijing Film Academy and starred in many films. In 1999, he directed his first film *Lunar Eclipse* and won the international jury award of the 22nd Moscow International Film Festival. His work *Tuya's Marriage* (2006) won the Golden Bear Award at the 57th Berlin International Film Festival. Wang Quan'an excels at integrating drama into realistic works, so that his works not only have humanistic care, paying attention to the downtrodden, especially the living conditions of Chinese women, but also have strong dramatic conflict and narrative tension. Wang Quan'an's shoots many works with Western Chinese themes, such as the Mongolian minority theme of *Tuya's Marriage*, *Weaving Girl* with Xi'an city as the background (2010) and the epic *White Deer Plain* (2012), showing a very distinctive regional style.

【手持摄影】 Hand-held photography

《白鹿原》中运用了大量的手持摄影，影片开端时，白嘉轩因听闻要交的皇粮被抢而跑出家门，以及鹿子霖告诉白嘉轩有人去县城闹事等情节，均利用手持摄影营造出大幅度的晃动感，将人物内心的焦急、不安以及紧张等情绪通过镜头传达给观众。同时，手持摄影所造成的镜头运动也加强了影片中的动感，增加了视觉冲击力。

A lot of hand-held photography is used in *White Deer Plain*. At the beginning of the film, Bai Jiaxuan ran out of his house because he heard that the imperial grain to be handed in was robbed, and Lu Zilin told Bai Jiaxuan that someone went to the county to make trouble. All of them use hand-held photography to create a large shaking movement and convey the anxiety and tension of the characters to the audience through the lens, strengthening the motion in the film and increasing the visual impact.

【长镜头】Long shot

本片开始便是长镜头拍摄起伏的麦浪，绵延不绝的麦田既交代了影片的空间——关中农村，也为影片奠定了恢宏大气的主要基调，营造了波澜壮阔的史诗氛围。片中多次运用"一镜一景"的镜头设计，长达 3 分钟的长镜头就有许多。例如影片结尾，已经疯掉的鹿子霖重新回到了白鹿原，日军的炮弹轰炸了白鹿原，这一过程用长镜头展现，凸显了冷静、客观的态度，将历史的残酷呈现在银幕之上。长镜头展现出村庄、麦田、冰河、夕阳之美，其所带来的影像真实和情感真实，是《白鹿原》的艺术特色之一。

At the beginning of the film, the rolling waves of wheat were filmed in a long shot. The endless wheat fields not only explained the space of the film—Guanzhong countryside, but also laid the main tone of the grand atmosphere for the film and created a magnificent epic atmosphere. The lens design of "one mirror and one scene" has been used many times in the film, and there are many long lenses up to 3 minutes. For example, at the end of the film, the crazy Lu Zilin returned to White Deer Plain while the Japanese bombed White Deer Plain. This process was shown in a long lens, highlighting a calm and objective attitude and presenting the cruelty of history on the screen. The long lens shows the beauty of villages, wheat fields, glaciers and sunset. The image reality and emotional reality it brings are one of the artistic features of *White Deer Plain*.

【文化象征】Cultural symbol

影片以金色麦浪开始，以金色麦浪结尾，导演用金黄色的麦浪象征陕西关中的土地。粮食是人类生存的必需品，人类的繁衍生息依附于土地之上，生老病死、婚丧嫁娶都有着土地的印记。无论朝代政权如何更迭，只有白鹿原这片神奇的土地始终占据着最重要的位置。影片中多次出现牌坊，牌坊是白鹿村的标志，是历史的见证，也隐喻着当时社会对女性的文化束缚，牌坊代表着中国传统的伦理道德——女性要遵守妇道，三从四德，从一而终。

The film starts with golden waves of wheat and ends with golden waves of wheat. The director uses golden waves of wheat to symbolize the land in Guanzhong, Shaanxi Province. Food is a necessity for human survival. Human reproduction depends on the land. Life, death, marriage and funerals have the mark of the land. No matter how the regime changes, only the magical land of White Deer Plain will still always occupy the most important position. The memorial archway appears many times in the film, which is the symbol of Bailu Village, the witness of history, and also a metaphor for the cultural constraints of society on women at that time. The memorial archway represents the traditional ethics of China, which indicates that women should abide by women's morality, three obediences and four virtues, and stick to one.

【戏曲元素】 Opera elements

影片中加入了许多民间戏曲的元素，起到了画龙点睛的作用，成为重要的文化符号和剧情线索。片中的关中戏曲元素主要有华阴老腔、碗碗腔、皮影以及秦腔。每当白鹿原上有大事发生，戏曲就配合着剧情出现，或悲怆，或激愤，为影片增添了民族史诗感和历史沧桑感。麦客们收完麦子以后在郭举人家大吼老腔《将令一声震山川》，气势磅礴，声音高亢，充满了男性的血性。这也和黑娃当时的状态不谋而合。当白孝文因为赌博输光了所有家产，和田小娥在一起时，插入了碗碗腔《桃源借水》的段落，田小娥一句"桃花源来了"把观众带入了皮影戏的故事中。片中的戏曲元素使影片散发出浓郁的陕西地域文化气息，视听语言成为塑造影片民族风格的重要手段。

Many elements of folk opera have been added to the film, which has played the role of the finishing touch and become an important cultural symbol and plot clue. Guanzhong opera elements in the film mainly include Huayin Lao Qiang, Wanwan Qiang, shadow play and Shaanxi Opera. Whenever something big happens in White Deer Plain, the opera appears with the plot, either pitiful or angry, adding a sense of national epic and historical vicissitudes to the film. After the wheat harvest, the wheat customers roared the Lao Qiang "General's Command" in Master Guo's house, which was magnificent, loud and full of courage and uprightness. This also coincides with Heiwa's state at that time. When Bai Xiaowen lost all his family property because of gambling and was with Tian Xiao'e, the paragraph of the Wanwan Qiang "Borrow Water from the Land of Peach Blossoms" is inserted. Tian Xiao'e's words "Here comes the Peach Garden" brought the audience into the story of shadow play. The opera elements in the film exude a strong flavor of Shaanxi regional culture, and the audio-visual language has become an important means to shape the national style of the film.

【田小娥形象】 Image of Tian Xiao'e

田小娥是影片中最具悲剧色彩的角色，作为片中唯一的女性主人公，田小娥的悲剧也是时代悲剧的缩影。封建社会的女性地位低下，田小娥嫁到举人家做三房姨太太，面对是没有性与爱的生活。当她和黑娃回到白鹿原后，却不被接纳，无法进入祠堂拜堂成亲，只能住在村外的窑洞里。黑娃逃走以后，面对生活的窘迫和世俗的眼光，只能被鹿子霖控制，去陷害白孝文。被鹿三杀害后，田小娥依然为世俗所不容，村民们修建了一座塔去压制田小娥的灵魂。田小娥的悲剧是时代造成的，她的个人命运影射着中国封建社会女性不能自由选择婚姻、无法获得个体独立的悲惨命运。

Tian Xiao'e is the most tragic character in the film. As the only female protagonist, Tian Xiao'e's tragedy also epitomizes the tragedy of the times. The status of women in feudal society was low. Tian Xiao'e was married as a third wife and faced a life without sexual activity and love. When she and Heiwa returned to White Deer Plain, they were not accepted and could not enter the ancestral hall to worship and marry. They had to live in a cave outside the village. After Heiwa escaped, facing the embarrassment of life and secular vision, he could only be controlled by Lu Zilin to frame Bai Xiaowen. After being killed by Lu San, Tian Xiao'e was still not tolerated by the secular world. The villagers built a tower to suppress Tian Xiao'e's soul. Tian Xiao'e's tragedy is a consequence of the times. Her personal fate reflects the tragic fate that women in Chinese feudal society could not freely choose marriage and obtain individual independence.

【鹿兆鹏】 Lu Zhaopeng

鹿兆鹏是鹿子霖的儿子，在影片中代表了新一代年轻人的思想观念和价值取向。鹿兆鹏加入了中国共产党，参加革命，接受马克思主义思想，勇于推翻旧社会的种种枷锁。鹿兆鹏能接受被村民们唾弃的黑娃和田小娥，并对他们宣讲了"婚姻自由"的观念。他抛下了封建包办婚姻制度下的妻子，加入了革命的浪潮之中，成为白鹿原这片土地上又一个"反叛者"。

Lu Zhaopeng, the son of Lu Zilin, represents the ideas and values of the new generation of young people in the film. Lu Zhaopeng joined the Communist Party of China, took part in the revolution, accepted Marxist thought, and had the courage to overthrow the shackles of the old society. Lu Zhaopeng accepted Heiwa and Tian Xiao'e, who were despised by the villagers, and preached the concept of "freedom of marriage" to them. He left his wife under the feudal arranged marriage system, joined the tide of revolution and became another "rebel" in the land of White Deer Plain.

互动讨论 Interactive discussion

1. 结合剧情和老师的讲解，试着讲讲你对这几句话的理解。

Try to explain your understanding of these sentences in combination with the plot and the teacher's explanation.

（1）老人：白鹿原是个好地方，你把我杀了你也拿不走。

Old man：White Deer Plain is a good place. Even if you kill me, you can't take it away.

（2）白嘉轩：子霖，你这闲话，能杀人。

Bai Jiaxuan：Zilin, you can kill people with your gossip.

2. 回答下列问题，并进行讨论。

Answer the following questions and discuss them.

（1）影片中，白嘉轩为什么不让黑娃和田小娥进入祠堂成亲？

In the film, why won't Bai Jiaxuan let Heiwa and Tian Xiao'e enter the ancestral hall to get married?

（2）在你的国家中，有没有具有史诗格局、反映国家变迁历史的影视作品？

In your country, are there any film and television works that have an epic pattern and reflect the history of national changes?

三、延伸阅读 Extended reading

1. 小说《白鹿原》The novel *White Deer Plain*

《白鹿原》是中国当代著名作家陈忠实的长篇小说，小说共计 50 余万字，写作 6 年后完成。《白鹿原》于 1993 年首次出版，1998 年获得中国第四届茅盾文学奖的殊荣。《白鹿原》具有宏大的历史背景和现实主义创作风格，通过对以陕西关中白鹿村中白姓、鹿姓两大家族之间半个多世纪恩怨纠葛的描写，展示了从清朝末年到二十世纪七八十年代中国的历史变迁，巧妙地将主人公们个人的命运和中国的历史进程相结合，被誉为"渭河平原五十年变迁的雄奇史诗"。小说《白鹿原》在中国影响力巨大，被改编成同名电影、电视剧、话剧、舞剧、秦腔等多种艺术形式。

（1）电视剧：电视剧版《白鹿原》，共计77集，于2016年推出。电视剧版更全面地展示了小说中的内容，再现了错综复杂的人物关系和时代变迁。

（2）话剧：经典版本有北京人民艺术剧院、陕西人民艺术剧院的版本，两个版本各有千秋，均获得了观众的好评。

（3）现代舞剧：舞剧版《白鹿原》用肢体语言带给观众纯美的艺术享受。

White Deer Plain is a novel written by Chen Zhongshi, a famous contemporary Chinese writer, with a total of more than 500,000 words. It took six years to complete. *White Deer Plain* was first published in 1993 and won the fourth Mao Dun Literature Award in 1998. *White Deer Plain* has a grand historical background and realistic creative style. Through the description of the grievances and entanglements between the Bai family and the Lu family in the White Deer Village in Guanzhong, Shaanxi Province for more than half a century, it shows the historical changes of China from the end of the Qing Dynasty to the 1970s and 1980s. It skillfully combines the personal fate of the protagonists with the historical process of China, and is known as "the magnificent epic of the changes of the Weihe Plain in the past 50 years". The novel *White Deer Plain* has had a great influence in China and has been adapted into a variety of artistic forms such as films, TV dramas, dramas, dance dramas, Shaanxi Opera and so on.

（1）TV dramas: the TV dramas version of *White Deer Plain*, had a total of 77 episodes, and was launched in 2016. The TV drama version shows the content of the novel more comprehensively, and reproduces the complex relationship between characters and the changes of the times.

（2）Dramas: the classic versions include Beijing People's Art Theatre and Shaanxi People's Art Theatre. Both versions have their own merits and have won high praise from the audience.

（3）Modern dance dramas: the dance dramas version of *White Deer Plain* uses body language to bring the audience pure and beautiful artistic enjoyment.

陈忠实 Chen Zhongshi

陈忠实于 1942 年出生于陕西西安，中国当代著名作家。代表作品有《接班以后》《蓝袍》《到老白杨树背后去》等。1980 年凭借《立身篇》获得飞天文学奖。长篇小说《白鹿原》获第四届茅盾文学奖。2009 年短篇小说《李十三推磨》获得第 13 届百花奖。2016 年 4 月，陈忠实因癌症在西安去世。陈忠实的小说多围绕家乡陕西进行写作，表现关中地区独特的风土人情和农民形象，关注历史中人和民族的命运，具有深刻的文化反思意识。

Chen Zhongshi was borned in 1942 in Xi'an, Shaanxi Province, who is a famous contemporary Chinese writer. Representative works include *After Taking Over*, *Blue Robe*, *Go Behind the Old Poplar Tree* and so on. In 1980, he won the Flying Literature Award for *Standing Up*. The novel *White Deer Plain* won the 4th Mao Dun Literature Award. In 2009, the short story *A Tale of Li Shisan and the Millstone* won the 13th Hundred Flowers Award. In April 2016, Chen Zhongshi died of cancer in Xi'an. Chen Zhongshi's novels are mostly set in his hometown, Shaanxi, showing the unique customs and depicting the image of farmers in Guanzhong area, paying attention to the fate of people and nations in history, and having a deep sense of cultural reflection.

白鹿原影视城 White Deer Plain Studios

白鹿原影视城位于陕西省西安市蓝田县，2016 年正式开园。该影视城主要为影视拍摄提供服务，并且可以供普通游客进行观光旅游，是集文化娱乐、休闲度假等功能于一体的综合性旅游区。主要景点有白鹿村、滋水县城、景观步道等，影视城的建筑风格以《白鹿原》小说中的关中民间建筑为主，在白鹿原影视城取景的有电影《百鸟朝凤》《老腔》，电视剧《白鹿原》《兵出潼关》等作品。白鹿原影视城还为游客提供大型真人特效特技实景剧《二虎守长安》、大型沉浸式"拍演放"一体化的演出《黑娃起义》、华阴老腔、杂技《白灵》等丰富多样的演出形式。

White Deer Plain Studios, located in Lantian County, Xi'an City, Shaanxi Province, was officially opened in 2016. The studios mainly provides services for film and television shooting and allow sightseeing for ordinary tourists. It is a comprehensive tourism area integrating cultural entertainment, leisure and vacation. The main scenic spots include Bailu

Village，Zishui County，landscape footpaths，etc. The architectural style of the studios is mainly based on the Guanzhong folk buildings in the novel *White Deer Plain*. The films *Song of the Phoenix*，*Yellow River Aria-Lao Qiang* and TV dramas *White Deer Plain* and *Soldiers Out of Tongguan* are taken in White Deer Plain Studios. White Deer Plain Studios also provides tourists with rich and diverse performances，such as the large-scale real-life special effect live show *Two Tigers Guarding Chang'an*，the large-scale immersive "shooting，performance and release" integrated performance *Heiwa Uprising*，Huayin Lao Qiang，and acrobatic *Bai Ling*.

2. 关中：帝王建都的风水宝地 Guanzhong：a geomantic treasure land where emperors built their capital

关中位于陕西省中部，包括西安市、宝鸡市、咸阳市、渭南市、铜川市，以及杨凌农业高新技术产业示范区。关中地区四面都有天然的屏障，易守难攻，所以秦、汉、隋、唐等朝代都将该地视为"龙兴之地"，不约而同地选择在关中的长安建立都城。关中平原物产丰饶，渭河从中穿越而过，其地理条件和气候条件适宜发展农业，是中国的风水宝地。关中地区文化旅游资源丰富，有兵马俑、华山、法门寺、太白山、黄帝陵、大雁塔等旅游景点。

Guanzhong is located in the middle of Shaanxi Province，including Xi'an City，Baoji City，Xianyang City，Weinan City，Tongchuan City，and Yangling agricultural high-tech industry demonstration zone. There are natural barriers on all sides of the Guanzhong area，which are easy to defend and difficult to attack. Therefore，the Qin，Han，Sui，Tang and other dynasties regarded the area as the "place of origin of a dynasty"，and spontaneously chose Chang'an in Guanzhong to establish the capital. Guanzhong Plain is rich in natural resources，and the Weihe River crosses it. Its geographical and climatic conditions are suitable for the development of agriculture. It is a geomantic treasure land in China. Guanzhong area is rich in cultural tourism resources，such as the Terracotta Warriors，Huashan Mountains，Famen Temple，Taibai Mountains，Huangdi Mausoleum and the Big Wild Goose Pagoda.

Biangbiang 面 BiangBiang Noodles

Biangbiang 面是关中传统面食，因为在制作时摔面发出的 biangbiang 声而得名。这是一种手擀面，面条厚实且非常宽，泼上油辣子，用大碗盛食。Biang 是一个合成字，在电脑中常用拼音替代。Biang 字在写作时有一个口诀：一点飞上天，黄河两道弯，八字大张口，言字往里走，左一扭，右一扭，你一长，我一长，当中夹个马大王，心作底，月作帮，搋个钉钉挂麻糖，推上车车逛咸阳。

Biangbiang Noodles is a traditional pasta in Guanzhong because of the noise emitted by slapping noodles during production. BiangBiang is named after this sound. It is a kind of handmade noodles. The noodles are thick and very wide. They are sprinkled with spicy oil and served in a large bowl. Biang is a synthetic word, which is often replaced by Pinyin in computers. There is a formula for writing the word "Biang": fly to heaven at one point, the Yellow River turns two corners, the eight characters open their mouth, the words go in, twist left and twist right, you grow and I grow, with a king horse in the middle, the heart as the bottom, the moon as the help, a nail to hang sesame sugar, push the car to Xianyang.

花馍 Huamo

陕西花馍起源于关中、陕北地区，是一种以面制作的花面馒头，通常被称为花馍或花面。人们利用简单的白面制作出了颜色鲜艳、造型多样、寓意和美的各式花色馍馍，主要用于逢年过节、婚丧嫁娶、祭祀祖先等民间节事活动中。

Shaanxi Huamo originated in Guanzhong and Northern Shaanxi. It is a kind of flowery steamed bun made of flour. It is usually called Huamo or Huamian. People use simple white flour to make all kinds of colorful steamed buns with bright colors, diverse shapes, moral and beauty, which are mainly used in folk festivals such as New Year holidays, weddings and funerals, sacrifices for ancestors and so on.

土织布 Local woven fabric

土织布是陕西民间广为传承的传统手工技法，陕西咸阳的武功县、乾县是其主要发源地。土织布由纯棉织成，经过 72 道工序纯手工制作，色彩艳丽，肤感舒适，具有浓郁的乡土气息和鲜明的民族特色。每逢嫁女，母亲都要为女儿亲手织出各色花样的床单作为嫁妆，并且把织布的技艺传给女儿，代代相传，这是中国人民勤劳和智慧的象征。

Local woven fabric is a traditional handicraft technique widely inherited by Shaanxi people, and its main birthplace is Wugong County and Qian County in Xianyang, Shaanxi Province. Local woven fabric is made of pure cotton and is handmade through 72 processes. It has bright colors, a comfortable skin feeling, strong local flavor and distinctive national characteristics. Every time a daughter is married, the mother will personally weave colorful sheets for her daughter as a dowry, and pass on the weaving skills to her daughter, carry on from generation to generation, which is a symbol of the diligence and wisdom of the Chinese people.

凤翔木板年画 Fengxiang wooden New Year pictures

陕西省宝鸡市凤翔区的木版年画是中国传统民间画中的重要流派，被誉为"东方智慧的结晶"。2006 年 5 月 20 日，凤翔木版年画入选第一批国家级非物质文化遗产名录。凤翔木版年画在唐宋时就已经开始创作，经历了民国时期，但是现今因为机器印刷的高效率和低成本，传统的木版年画手艺几乎中断。凤翔木版年画的题材主要有风俗画、家宅六神、窗花画等。

The wooden New Year pictures in Fengxiang District, Baoji City, Shaanxi Province is an important genre of traditional Chinese folk painting, known as "the crystallization of Oriental wisdom". On May 20, 2006, Fengxiang wooden New Year pictures were selected into the first batch of National Intangible Cultural Heritage List. Fengxiang wooden New Year pictures began to be created in the Tang and Song Dynasties and experienced the period of the Republic of China, but now the traditional technology of wooden New Year pictures is almost extinct because of the high efficiency and low cost of machine printing. The themes of Fengxiang wooden New Year pictures mainly include custom paintings, six gods of family houses, window flower paintings, etc.

陕西八大怪 Eight customs of Shaanxi

又称"关中八大怪"，主要是指陕西关中地区出现的八种独特的传统习俗。分别是，第一怪：板凳不坐蹲起来；第二怪：房子半边盖；第三怪：盆碗不分开；第四怪：帕帕头上戴；第五怪：面条像裤带；第六怪：锅盔像锅盖；第七怪：油泼辣子一道菜；第八怪：秦腔不唱吼起来。

Also known as "Eight customs of Guanzhong", mainly refers to eight unique traditional customs in Guanzhong, Shaanxi Province. Respectively, the first custom：people do not sit on the bench but squat on it; The second custom：only half of the house is built; The third custom：pots and bowls are not separated; The fourth custom：wearing a handkerchief on the head; The fifth custom：noodles are like trouser belts; The sixth custom：a pot helmet is like a pot lid; The seventh custom：pour spicy oil on the plate and a dish is made; The eighth custom：Shaanxi Opera is not sung, it is roared.

四、课后思考 After class thinking

1. 通过电影《白鹿原》和延伸阅读的学习，简单描述你对陕西关中的印象。

Briefly describe your impression of Guanzhong, Shaanxi Province, through the study of the film *White Deer Plain* and extended reading.

2. 和大家分享一下，在你的国家，有哪些具有地域特色的美食？

What is the local cuisine of your country? Share it with the class.

五、互动时间 Interaction time

一起来学习陕西方言吧！

Let's learn Shaanxi dialect together!

么马达：没问题，一般表示自己可以顺利地做完某事。

克里马擦：表示动作麻利、干活迅速，干脆利落地做完某事。

聊咋咧：太好了、非常好。表示开心与赞同。

谝闲传：聊天，多指对于不重要事情的讨论和闲聊。

咥一碗：咥就是吃的意思，咥一碗就是吃一碗，通常指的是吃面。

扎式：摆架子，打肿脸充胖子的意思。

哈怂：指的是坏人。

木乱：麻烦、思绪烦乱的意思。

Me ma da：No problem. It usually means that you can finish something smoothly.

Ke li ma ca：It means to move quickly, work quickly, and finish something quickly.

Liao za lie：It means great, very good. Express happiness and approval.

Pian xian chuan：Chatting, it refers to discuss about unimportant things.

Die yi wan：Die means eating. Die yi wan means eating a bowl. It usually refers to eating noodles.

Zha shi：It means put on airs slap one's face until it's swollen in an effort to look imposing.

Ha song：It refers to bad people.

Mu luan：It means trouble, confused thoughts.

第三单元
双旗镇刀客

本单元重点

1.了解电影《双旗镇刀客》的艺术特色
2.了解中国"侠文化"的基本知识

本单元难点

1.了解电影中的侠客形象
2.了解电影《双旗镇刀客》和传统武侠片的不同之处

Unit 3
The Swordsman in Double Flag Town

 Key points

1.Learn about the artistic characteristics of *The Swordsman in Double Flag Town*

2.Learn about the basic knowledge of Chinese "martial arts culture"

 Difficult points

1.Know about the swordsman depicted in this film

2.Know about the differences between *The Swordsman in Double Flag Town* and other conventional martial arts films

《双旗镇刀客》：武侠片新范式

The Swordsman in Double Flag Town：A New Model of Martial Arts Films

一、丝路放映厅 Silk Road screen hall

导演：何平

编剧：何平/杨争光

主演：高一玮/赵玛娜/常江/孙海英/王刚

类型：动作/冒险/武侠

制片国家/地区：中国大陆

上映日期：1991－05－17（中国大陆）

片长：90 分钟

英文名：*The Swordsman in Double Flag Town*

Director：He Ping

Screenwriter：He Ping/Yang Zhengguang

Starring：Gao Yiwei/Zhao Mana/Chang Jiang/Sun Haiying/Wang Gang

Type：Action/Adventure/Martial Arts

Producer countries/regions：Chinese mainland

Release date：May 17，1991（Chinese mainland）

Length：90 minutes

English name：*The Swordsman in Double Flag Town*

主要获奖 Major awards

第 11 届中国电影金鸡奖：最佳美术

第 11 届香港电影金像奖：十大华语片

第 43 届柏林国际电影节：国际影评奖

The 11th China Film Golden Rooster Award：Best Art

The 11th Hong Kong Film Award：Top Ten Chinese Films

The 43rd Berlin International Film Festival：International Film Review Award

剧情梗概 Plot synopsis

故事发生在人烟稀少、黄沙漫天的中国西北部。男主角孩哥（高一玮饰）是一个十四五岁的孩子，他爹临死前跟他说有个娃娃亲，叫他去双旗镇娶未过门的媳妇，于是孩哥踏上了自己的娶妻之路。

路上，孩哥遇到了颇有威望的大侠沙里飞。孩哥与其结交，沙里飞临走时还借走了孩哥一半的彩礼钱，并承诺有事找他。孩哥来到双旗镇时遇到了两个蒙面刀客，正在寻找一个叫"一刀仙"的土匪，当时大漠里土匪横行，百姓生活得异常艰苦。孩哥在双旗镇找到了老丈人瘸子和未过门的媳妇好妹，可是瘸子看孩哥一个小孩，又没本事，便想悔婚。直到孩哥展现出了自己的刀法，才让他们另眼相待。这天，一刀仙的弟弟在饭馆喝酒，看中了好妹，图谋不轨。孩哥出手相救出刀杀死了他，小镇上的人都吓坏了，因为他们知道一刀仙肯定会来报仇。当晚，瘸子就把好妹嫁给了孩哥，第二天孩哥带着好妹准备逃跑避难，村民们却要孩哥留下，他们害怕一刀仙的报复。孩哥去找了大侠沙里飞，谁知沙里飞却在一刀仙到来时不见踪影，意识到被骗的孩哥决定独自承担。小镇上的人冷漠地看着，只有三个人挺身而出，孩哥也拔出了刀，最终，一刀仙死在了孩哥的刀下，孩哥与好妹就此离开小镇。

The story takes place in the sparsely populated and desert-area northwest of China. The hero, Hai Ge (played by Gao Yiwei), is a 14 or 15-year-old child. Before his father's death, his father told him that he had found him a child marriage and asked him to go to Double Flag Town to marry her, so Hai Ge went to find his fiancée.

On the way, Hai Ge met the great swordsman Sha Lifei, who had prestige. Hai Ge made friends with him. Sha Lifei borrowed half of the betrothal gifts from Hai Ge and promised that if Hai Ge had any problems to come to find him, and then he left. When Hai Ge went to Double Flag Town, he met two masked swordsmen who were looking for a bandit named "Yi Daoxian". At that time, bandits were widespread in the desert and people lived an extremely hard life. Hai Ge found out his lame father-in-law and his fiancée, Hao Mei. But the lame father-in-law thought Hai Ge was just a child and not capable enough to marry his daughter. It was not until Hai Ge showed his sword skills that he began to view him in a different light. That day, Yi Daoxian's younger brother drank in a restaurant, looked at Hao Mei and had malicious intents. Hai Ge saved her and killed him with a sword. The people in the town were terrified because they knew that Yi Daoxian would come for revenge. That night, the lame man let Hai Ge marry Hao Mei. The next day, Hai Ge and Hao Mei were ready to escape and take refuge, but the villagers asked Hai Ge to stay. They were afraid of revenge from Yi Daoxian. Hai Ge went to find the great swordsman Sha Lifei, but Sha Lifei disappeared when Yi Daoxian came. Hai Ge realized that he was cheated and decided to bear it alone. The people in the town looked indifferently. Only three people came forward and Hai Ge also pulled out the sword. Finally, Yi Daoxian died by Hai Ge's sword. Hai Ge and Hao Mei then left the town.

重要词汇 Important vocabularies

娃娃亲	wá·waqīn	*n.*	child marriage
威望	wēiwàng	*n.*	prestige
彩礼	cǎilǐ	*n.*	betrothal gifts
承诺	chéngnuò	*v.*	promise
报仇	bào//chóu	*v.*	revenge
冷漠	lěngmò	*adj.*	indifferent

例句 Example sentences

1. 在他很小的时候，父母就给他定了娃娃亲。

When he was very young, his parents contracted him in a child marriage.

2. 作为一名退休干部，他在当地十分有威望。

As a retired cadre, he had great prestige in the local area.

3. 如果没有彩礼，很难把妻子娶进门。

With no betrothal gifts, it is difficult to take a wife.

4. 空口无凭的承诺往往都不可信。

Empty promises are often unreliable.

5. 中国有句古话：君子报仇，十年不晚。

There is an old Chinese saying: it is never too late for a man to take revenge.

6. 二十年的艰难经历让他看起来非常冷漠。

Twenty years of hard experience made him look very indifferent.

语言练习 Language practices

请为以下句子选择合适的词语进行填空。

Please fill in the blanks with the appropriate words for the following sentences.

1. 爷爷善良淳朴，在村子里有很高的（   ）。

Grandpa is kind and honest and has a high (   ) in the village.

2. 你必须隐藏身份，以防他回来（   ）。

You must hide your identity in case he comes back for (   ).

3. （   ）是中国传统婚嫁习俗中的一部分。

(   ) is a part of Chinese traditional marriage customs.

4. 他外表很（   ），但内心十分热情。

He looks very (   ), but his heart is very enthusiastic.

5. 现代社会已经不提倡（   ），阻碍婚姻自由。

Modern society does not advocate (   ), because it hinders the freedom of marriage.

6. 他向我（   ），一定会加倍努力。

He (   ) to me that he would work harder.

二、丝路大讲堂 Silk Road lecture hall

【导演特色】 Featuring director

何平，1957 年 10 月出生于山西。代表作品有《川岛芳子》（1987 年）、《双旗镇刀客》（1991 年）、《炮打双灯》（1994 年）、《天地英雄》（2003 年）、《麦田》（2009 年）

等。何平导演用影像讲述了一个乡土的中国，用武侠精神和西部情结支撑了他的作品风格。他的影像设计独到用心，体现出独树一帜的视觉风格。从《双旗镇刀客》开始，影像就在他的电影里中起着举足轻重的作用，在何平导演的电影中，视觉的元素被无限地放大，承载着叙事和表意的双重功能。剪辑上采用"只见动势不见动作"的方法进行武打动作的展现，给观众营造出一定的想象空间，享受由视觉所带来的电影魅力。

He Ping was born in Shanxi in October 1957. His representative works include *Kawashima Yoshiko* （1987）, *The Swordsman in Double Flag Town* （1991）, *Red Firecracker*, *Green Firecracker* （1994）, *Warriors of Heaven and Earth* （2003）, *Wheat* （2009）, etc. Director He Ping described the images of rural China and added to his work style the martial arts spirit and western complexity. His image design has unique details and a unique visual style. Since directing *The Swordsman in Double Flag Town*, images have played an important role in his films. In the films directed by He Ping, the visual elements are infinitely enlarged, serving the dual functions of narration and ideography. The editing adopts the method of "seeing the momentum but not the action" to show the martial arts action, so as to create a certain imagination space for the audience and enjoy the film charm brought by vision.

【视觉风格】 Visual style

西北的戈壁荒漠和破败的穷僻小镇是影片的主要视觉场景。当马蹄踏破黄沙迎风而起，塞漠孤烟映照出人物的剪影效果，影片营造出一种孤寂压抑之感。黄色作为影片的主色调，与棕色、黑色相搭配，构成了一副荒芜的小镇景象。镜头将人物置身于萧瑟的环境里，人物造型的蓬头垢面、衣衫褴褛就显得尤为契合。大漠、沙丘、骆驼城遗址在导演的镜头下充满了诗意和活力，影片开头展示了夕阳下的大漠，孩哥骑着马在大漠中奔驰，雄浑壮美，使影片具备了诗意风格。

The Gobi Desert in the northwest and the ruined and poor town are the main focal points of the film. When the horseshoe breaks through the yellow sand and rises in the wind, the lonely smoke in the desert reflects the silhouette effect of the characters and the film creates a sense of loneliness and depression. As the main color of the film, yellow is matched with brown and black to form a desolate town scene. The camera places the characters in a bleak environment. The messy hair and dirty face and ragged clothes of the characters are particularly suitable for the effects. The desert, sand dunes and camel city ruins are full of poetry and vitality under the director's lens. At the beginning of the film, the desert under the setting sun is displayed. Hai Ge rides his horse in the splendid desert, evoking a poetic style.

【人物刻画】 Characterization

影片中刻画了三位男性人物形象：孩哥、沙里飞、一刀仙，三人都与传统武侠片中的英雄人物形象大相径庭。传统武侠片中的主角往往是胸怀天下、忠肝义胆的大侠或者英雄。

影片中的主角孩哥只是一个十几岁的涉世未深的孩子，其所有的行动都非主观意愿，外部环境的压迫致使他被卷入一系列事件中。他来双旗镇迎娶好妹是父亲的夙愿，一刀仙的弟弟强暴好妹时他被迫出手，最后与一刀仙决战也是无奈之举，虽然他成功战胜了一刀仙，但并不是出于人物的自觉意志。沙里飞在江湖中颇有名气，是百姓口中的大侠。他表面上义薄云天，但其实"金玉其外，败絮其中"，根本没有匹配名气的实力。他刚遇到孩哥时就骗了一半的彩礼钱，并夸下海口，之后更是骗孩哥会来迎战一刀仙，结果观望至战斗结束时才假惺惺来装模作样，最后还拿走了属于孩哥的战利品，他是虚伪人性的典型。讽刺的是，反派一刀仙竟是这部影片中最具有英雄气质的主角。他虽是土匪，但做事充满着一股侠义之气和江湖作风，他为了帮兄弟报仇甚至不惜牺牲自己的生命。

The film depicts three male characters: Hai Ge, Sha Lifei and Yi Daoxian. They are all very different from the heroes in traditional martial arts films. The protagonist in traditional martial arts films is often a great swordsman or a hero who has humanity in his mind and is loyal and courageous.

The protagonist of the film, Hai Ge, is just in his teens, who has not been deeply involved in the world. All his actions are not subjective. But the adverse circumstances have led him to be involved in a series of events. It was his father's long cherished wish that he came to the Double Flag Town to marry Hao Mei. When Yi Daoxian's younger brother violently took Hao Mei, he was forced to fight. In the end, he had no choice but to fight with Yi Daoxian. Although he successfully defeated Yi Daoxian, it was against his better judgement. Sha Lifei was very famous in the Jianghu as a great and admired swordsman. On the surface, his high morality reaches up to the clouds, but in fact his fame does not match the reality.

When he first met Hai Ge, he directly cheated Hai Ge out of half of the betrothal gifts. Later, he tricked Hai Ge again into coming to fight against Yi Daoxian and just pretended he would join the fight, but he didn't. Finally, he took away the war trophies of Hai Ge. He epitomized hypocrisy. Ironically, the villain Yi Daoxian is the most heroic protagonist in the film. Although he is a bandit, his work is full of chivalry and Jianghu style. In order to avenge his brother, he even sacrificed his life.

【武侠片的反类型】 Anti genre of martial arts films

中国的武侠片起源于 20 世纪 20 年代末期的上海，到了 70 年代在香港大放光彩，出现了李小龙、成龙等武打明星。80 年代到 90 年代，香港再创新武侠风潮，李连杰、甄子丹、赵文卓等武打明星应运而生。传统武侠电影动作场面上主要有两种风格：第一种是以特技为主的仙侠题材，动作设计上注重飘逸、唯美。第二种是硬桥硬马的写实武打片，以真打实拍为主，突出技巧性。本片中的动作场景另辟蹊径，并没有突出动作美感或着重展现暴力场面，而是借鉴了美国西部片枪战场景的简洁剪辑方式，与中国武侠电影形成了反差。另外，本片中"反英雄"的人物设定，也与武侠片中行侠仗义、热血爱国的正派英雄形象形成了对比。

Chinese martial arts films originated in Shanghai in the late 1920s. In the 1970s, they flourished in Hong Kong, with martial arts stars such as Bruce Lee and Jackie Chan. From the 1980s to the 1990s, Hong Kong renewed the trend of martial arts, and martial arts stars such as Jet Li, Donnie Yen and Zhao Wenzhuo became famous. There are two main styles in the action scenes of traditional martial arts films: the first is the celestial swordsman theme based on special effects, and the action design centered on elegance and aestheticism. The second is the realistic and raw martial arts films, which focuses on real shooting and highlights skills. The action scenes in these types of films are different. This film does not highlight the beauty of action or focus on the violent scenes, but draws on the tradition of the concise editing method of gun battle scenes in American Westerns, which forms a contrast with Chinese martial arts films. In addition, the character setting of the "anti-hero" in this film also forms a contrast with the righteous hero image of chivalry and patriotism in the martial arts film.

【动作风格】 Action style

本片以极其平静写意的手法触及江湖仇杀的爱恨情仇。镜头上简洁明快，人物动作干净利落，以"留白"手法营造出意境。影片的高潮部分将暴力美学使用到了极致，主角孩哥已经到了最危急的时刻，他与一刀仙对峙，镜头展现两人打斗的画面，观众只能从刀划破空气的音爆声和扬起的黄沙去猜测结果。直到一刀仙倒在地上，孩哥满脸是血，观众突然发现这场大决战已经结束。孩哥获胜的结局在意料之外又在情理之中，西北刀客刀术的神奇也得以充分展现。

This film calmly and simply displays the love and hate of Jianghu' revenge. The lens is concise and lively, and the action of the characters is clean and neat. The artistic conception is created by the "leaving blank" effect. The climax of the film pushes the aesthetics of violence to the extreme. The protagonist, Hai Ge, has reached the most critical moment where he confronts Yi Daoxian. The shot shows the picture of two people fighting. The audience, hearing only the swish of the sword cutting through the air can only guess at the outcome. Until, suddenly they see Yi Daoxian fall to the ground, Hai Ge's face is covered with blood and the fight is over. Hai Ge's victory was unexpected but satisfying. In this way the magic of the Northwest swordsman's skill was fully demonstrated.

【看客群像】 Audience portrait

《双旗镇刀客》中除了围绕三个刀客主人公所展开的主线剧情外，还着重刻画了小镇居民的人物群像。小镇上的居民看上去老实本分，平日里秉持"各人自扫门前雪，莫管他人瓦上霜"的态度，生活十分安逸。当二爷想要强暴好妹时，居民的默不作声；当孩哥杀死了二当家后，因为害怕"一刀仙"的报复便对孩哥恶语相加，不让他逃跑；当孩哥搬出了"沙里飞"的大名后，又与孩哥把酒言欢；当"一刀仙"来寻仇时，镇子上的大部分人成为冷漠的看客，不愿意相助。对镇上居民的塑造，讽刺了暴政下自私自利、麻木不仁、"沉默的大多数"的集体形象。

In *The Swordsman in Double Flag Town*, in addition to the main plot around the three swordsman heroes, the story also focuses on the portraits of the town residents. The residents of the town seem to be honest and dutiful. On weekdays, they follow the attitude of "everyone sweeps the snow in front of the door and doesn't care about the frost on others' tiles". Their life is very comfortable. When Er Ye wanted to abuse Hao Mei, people kept silent. But when Hai Ge killed Er Ye, people were afraid of the revenge of Yi Daoxian, so they started to curse him and wouldn't let him escape. When Hai Ge spoke the eminent name of "Sha Lifei", they had another drink with him. When Yi Daoxian came to seek revenge, most people in the town became indifferent spectators and were unwilling to help. The portrayal of the town residents satirizes the collective image of the selfish and insensitive and "silent mass" under tyranny.

互动讨论 Interactive discussion

1. 结合剧情和老师的讲解，试着讲讲你对这几个问题的理解。

Explain your understanding of these questions in combination with the plot and the teacher's explanation.

（1）试着解释"孩哥""沙里飞""一刀仙"这三个人名字的含义。

What do you think is the meaning of the names of "Hai Ge", "Sha Lifei" and "Yi Daoxian"?

（2）造成小镇人们成为看客的原因是什么？

Why do you think people in small towns become indifferent spectators?

2. 回答以下问题，并进行讨论。

Answer and discuss the following questions.

（1）本片中的英雄和你了解的武侠片中的英雄有何异同？

What are the differences and similarities between the heroes in this film and the heroes in martial arts films that you know?

（2）在你的国家，有哪些侠客的传奇故事，试着举出一两个例子。

What are the legends of chivalrous men in your country? Try to give one or two examples.

三、延伸阅读 Extended reading

1. 西安电影制片厂与西部电影 Xi'an Film Studio and Western films

西安电影制片厂于 1956 年 4 月筹建，1958 年 8 月正式成立。西安电影制片厂位于陕西西安，坐落于世界闻名的大雁塔旁西影路 508 号。20 世纪 80 年代，西安电影制片厂在第三任厂长吴天明的领导下发展迅速，成为国有体制下中国八大电影制片厂之首。导演出身的吴天明大胆起用新人，发掘并培养了张艺谋、陈凯歌、顾长卫等著名的

"第五代"导演，随着《黄土地》《红高粱》《双旗镇刀客》等影片的问世和获奖，西安电影制片厂开启了前所未有的繁荣时期。随着中国经济市场的发展，西安电影制片厂也在积极转型。2000 年 6 月，西安电影制片厂成为股份有限公司。2009 年 5 月，西安电影制片厂成为西部电影集团有限公司。现在的西安电影制片厂积极地适应时代变化，成立了西影电影艺术体验中心，游客可以在电影制作技术科普体验区、大话西游奇妙屋等各类特色展馆中感受电影的魅力。另外，西安电影制片厂也宣布与西北大学、陕文投集团共同建设西安电影学院。

Xi'an Film Studio, was created in April 1956 and officially established in August 1958. Xi'an Film Studio is located in Xi'an, Shaanxi Province, at 508 Xiying Road next to the world-famous Big Wild Goose Pagoda. In the 1980s, Xi'an Film Studio developed rapidly under the leadership of Wu Tianming, the third director, and became the first of China's eight film studios under the state-owned system. Wu Tianming, who was rising as a director, dared to hire new people. He discovered and trained the famous fifth generation of film directors such as Zhang Yimou, Chen Kaige and Gu Changwei. With the advent and awards of films such as *Yellow Earth*, *Red Sorghum* and *The Swordsman in Double Flag Town*, Xi'an Film Studio has enjoyed an unprecedented period of success. With the development of China's economic market, Xi'an Film Studio was also expanded and transformed. In June 2000, Xi'an Film Studio became a joint stock company, and in May 2009, it became a Western Film Group Co., Ltd. The current Western Film Studio actively adapts to the changes of the times and has established a Western Film Art Experience Center. Tourists can feel the charm of the film in various characteristic pavilions such as the popular science experience area of film production technology and the wonderful house of A Chinese Odyssey. In addition, Xi'an Film Studio also announced their cooperation with the Northwest University and the Shaanxi Culture Investment Group for the joint construction of a Xi'an Film Faculty.

西安电影制片厂代表作品 Representative works of Xi'an Film Studio

西安电影制片厂建厂至今已有 60 余年历史，为中国电影培养出了诸多优秀的导演、演员、摄影、编剧等人才，也为中国电影创作出许多经典作品：

（1）《老井》（1987 年）：导演吴天明，影片讲述了年轻人孙旺泉带领村民对抗恶劣的西部自然条件，在科学的帮助下，为几百年来缺水的老井村成功打出水井的故事。

本片在 1987 年第 2 届日本东京国际电影节上获得最佳故事片金麒麟奖，拉开了西安电影制片厂辉煌的序幕。

（2）《炮打双灯》（1994 年）：导演何平，影片讲述了女扮男装的大户小姐与画匠之间跨越阶级的爱情悲剧。本片获得第 14 届金鸡奖最佳男女主角、最佳男配角、最佳摄影。

（3）《美丽的大脚》（2003 年）：导演杨亚洲，影片讲述了贫穷山村的一位模范老师张美丽的故事。当张美丽与城里来的志愿者夏雨解除了误会，为了山区脱贫致富、为了孩子们的未来共同努力时，张美丽却意外离世。本片获得第 22 届中国电影金鸡奖最佳故事片、最佳导演、最佳女主角、最佳女配角。

（4）《图雅的婚事》（2007 年）：导演王全安，影片以中国蒙古族为背景，展示了中国西部草原上的人与事。受伤的图雅不能再靠劳动维持生计，只能带着已经瘫痪的丈夫和孩子改嫁，图雅的正直善良赢得了很多人的追求，而"嫁夫养夫"的执着却不能为大家所接受。本片在第 57 届柏林电影节上获得最佳影片奖，即金熊奖。

Xi'an Film Studio has a history going back more than 60 years. It has trained many excellent directors, actors, photographers, screenwriters and other talents for Chinese films and also created many classic works for Chinese films:

（1）*Old Well* (1987): directed by Wu Tianming. The film tells the story of a young man, Sun Wangquan, who with the help of science, led the villagers to overcome the water shortage which had persisted for hundreds of years, by successfully drilling the well. The film won the Golden Kirin Award for Best Feature Film at the 2nd Tokyo International Film Festival in 1987, which debuted the glory of Xi'an Film Studio.

（2）*Red Firecracker, Green Firecracker* (1994): directed by He Ping. The film tells the story of a class-crossing love tragedy between a woman dressed as a man and a painter. This film won the 14th Golden Rooster Award for Best Actor and Actress, Best Supporting Actor and Best Photography.

（3）*Pretty Big Feet* (2003): directed by Yang Yazhou. The film tells the story of Zhang Meili, a exemplary teacher in a poor mountain village. Zhang Meili and Xia Yu, a volunteer from the city, cleared up the misunderstanding and worked together to get rid of poverty and got rich in the mountain area and when they were striving to assure the future of the children, Zhang Meili died unexpectedly. The film won the Best Feature Film, Best Director, Best Actress and Best Supporting Actress of the 22nd China Film Golden Rooster Award.

(4) *Tuya's Marriage* (2007): directed by Wang Quan'an. The film shows the people and things on the grassland in Western China against the backdrop of the Chinese Mongol minority. The injured Tuya can no longer rely on labor to make a living and can only re-marry with her paralyzed husband and children. Tuya's integrity and kindness won the support of many people, but the persistence of "marrying the second man and raising her first husband" cannot be accepted by everyone. The film won the Best Film Award, i. e., the Golden Bear Award, at the 57th Berlin Film Festival.

中国西部电影 Western Chinese films

西安电影制片厂曾经代表着华语电影的最高成就，也孕育出中国电影历史上的著名电影流派——中国西部电影。中国西部电影与美国西部电影不同，并不是一种商业类型片，而是出现在 1984 年以后，以中国西部为背景，反映西部地区人民生活状况和生存状态，具有西部精神和深厚文化内涵的电影流派。中国西部电影是具有强烈民族个性色彩的电影。

Xi'an Film Studio not only represented the highest achievement of Chinese films but also gave birth to the most popular film genre in Chinese film history—the Western Chinese films. Different from Western American films, Western Chinese films are not a commercial type of film, but a film genre with western spirit and profound cultural connotation, which appeared after 1984. It takes Western China as the background and reflects the living conditions and status quo of the people in the western region. Western Chinese films are films with a strong national personality.

2. 镇北堡西部影城 Zhenbeibu China West Film Studio

电影《双旗镇刀客》中苍凉、雄浑的北方景观，主要取景于镇北堡西部影城。它坐落于中国宁夏回族自治区贺兰山麓，是中国十大影视基地之一，由著名作家张贤亮于 1993 年创办。目前，镇北堡西部影城已经发展为集休闲、娱乐、观光、餐饮于一体的旅游胜地，被评为 5A 级旅游景区、亚洲品牌 500 强，被誉为"宁夏之宝"。镇北堡西部影城分为镇北堡和镇南堡两个古代城堡，整个影城具有非常强烈的民间特色，整体景观苍凉、古朴、原始，具有中国西部风格。《红高粱》《大话西游》《新龙门客栈》《牧马人》《刺陵》等诸多华语电影均在此拍摄。西部影城主要有老银川一条街、明城、清城三个文化板块，建设有影视片重要场景 200 余处，复原的一些经典电影场景，比如《大话西游》中的盘丝洞和城楼，电影《红高粱》中的"月亮坡"和酿酒作坊等经典场景都是游客必去的景点。镇北堡西部影城在保护文物的基础上，对中国物质遗产和非物质文化遗产都有了传承与发扬，在几乎是废墟的古堡上让中国电影走向世界，镇北堡的成功是现代文化产业发展的代表。

The bleak and rugged northern landscape in the film *The Swordsman in Double Flag Town* is mainly set in the Zhenbeibu China West Film Studio. It is located at the foot of Helan Mountain in Ningxia Hui Autonomous Region, China. It is one of the top ten film and television bases in China. It was founded by the famous writer Zhang Xianliang in 1993. At present, Zhenbeibu China West Film Studio has developed into a tourist attraction integrating leisure, entertainment, sightseeing and catering. It has been rated as a 5A tourist attraction and one of the top 500 Asian brands and is known as the "treasure of Ningxia". Zhenbeibu China West Film Studio is divided into two ancient castles, Zhenbeibu and Zhennanbu. The whole cinema has very strong folk characteristics. Overall, the landscape is desolate, simple and primitive, redolent with the style of Western China. Many Chinese films such as *Red Sorghum*, *A Chinese Odyssey*, *New Dragon Gate Inn*, *The Herdsman* and *The Treasure Hunter* were filmed on location here. There are three cultural sections of the Studio, namely, Laoyinchuan Street, Mingcheng and Qingcheng. There are more than 200 important scenes of film and television films. Some of the restored classic film scenes, such as the cave of the silken web and the city tower in the film *A Chinese Odyssey*, the "moon slope" in the film *Red Sorghum* and the wine making workshop, are all tourist attractions. On the basis of protecting cultural relics, Zhenbeibu China West Film Studio has inherited and carried forward China's material and intangible cultural heritage. Let Chinese films go to the world on the patricidal ruins of the ancient castle, Zhenbeibu's success is the representative of the development of modern cultural industry.

3. 武侠电影 Martial arts films

武侠电影 Martial arts films

武侠电影是中国独有的电影类型，也是世界上影响力最大的电影类型之一，又名功夫片。中国武侠电影吸取了戏曲、文学、武术中的精华，并且借鉴了西方动作电影和喜剧电影的表演形式，形成了以中国武侠文学为原型、表现人物武打动作的类型电影。中国著名的武侠形象有霍元甲、张三丰、黄飞鸿、叶问等，武打明星有李小龙、成龙、李连杰、吴京等，武侠电影代表作有《精武门》（1972 年）、《蛇形刁手》（1978 年）、《少林寺》（1982 年）、《黄飞鸿》系列、《一代宗师》（2013 年）等。

Martial arts films is a unique film type in China and one of the most influential film types in the world. It is also known as Kung Fu films. China's martial arts films portray the essence of drama, literature and martial arts, and use the form of western action movies and comedy films to form China's martial arts literature as the prototype, and to display the martial arts genre. Famous martial arts films in China include Huo Yuanjia, Zhang Sanfeng, Huang Feihong, Ye Wen, etc. Martial arts stars include Bruce Lee, Jackie Chan, Jet Li, Wu Jing, etc. Martial arts films masterpieces include *Fist of Fury* (1972), *Snake in the Eagle's Shadow* (1978), *The Shaolin Temple* (1982), *Wong Fei-Hung* series, *The Grandmaster* (2013), etc.

武侠文化 Martial arts culture

武侠文化产生于封建时代，揭示了底层人民在专制统治下崇尚自由的人格与文化精神。中国历史中的侠客敢于利用薄弱的力量去挑战集体的、宏大的权威和不合理的现实社会秩序，在中国人民心里留下了美好印象，并且逐步积淀为一种重要的文化行为和期待心理，在民间传说、武侠文学和武侠电影中树立了诸多英雄和侠客的形象。他们注重承诺，遵守信用，不惜性命为百姓打抱不平，甚至与国家权力作斗争，成为民众心中正义的化身。

Martial arts culture originated from the feudal era and revealed the personality and cultural spirit of the common people advocating freedom under the autocratic rule. Chivalrous men in Chinese history dare to use their weak strength to challenge the collective unreasonableness of authoritarian social order. They have left a good impression in the hearts of the Chinese people and have gradually developed into an important cultural behavior and expectation psychology. They have established many images of heroes and chivalrous men in the folklore, martial arts literature and martial arts films. They pay attention to commitment, loyalty, fight injustice for the people at all costs and even fight against state power, becoming the embodiment of justice in the hearts of the people.

四、课后思考 After class thinking

1. 通过电影《双旗镇刀客》和此节内容的学习，简述你对武侠文化的认识。

Briefly describe your understanding of martial arts culture through the film *The Swordsman in Double Flag Town* and the study of this section.

2. 你最喜欢的武侠电影是哪部？你认为中国的侠客和漫画中的超人、复仇者联盟形象有何不同？

What is your favorite martial arts film? What do you think is the difference between Chinese chivalrous men and the image of Superman and the Avengers in the comics?

五、互动时间 Interaction time

欣赏并学习演唱歌曲《醉拳》，这首歌是成龙主演电影《醉拳2》（1994 年）的主题曲。

Enjoy and learn to sing the song "Drunken Master", which is the theme song of Jackie Chan's film *Drunken Master 2*（1994）.

醉　拳

作词：厉曼婷

作曲：李偲菘、李伟菘

演唱：成龙

我颠颠又倒倒　好比浪涛

有万种的委屈　付之一笑

我一下低　我一下高

摇摇晃晃不肯倒

酒里乾坤我最知道

江湖中闯名号　从来不用刀

千斤的重担我一肩挑

不喊冤也不求饶

对情意我肯弯腰

醉中仙好汉一条

莫说狂　狂人心存厚道

莫笑痴　因痴心难找

莫怕醉　醉过海阔天高

且狂且痴且醉趁年少

Drunken Master

Lyricist：Li Manting

Composer：Li Sisong，Li Weisong

Singer：Jackie Chan

I stumble and fall like a wave

There are thousands of grievances to dismiss with a laugh

I'm low and I'm high

I stagger but refuse to fall

The world of wine I know better

You never use a sword to gain fame in Jianghu

I carry a heavy burden of kilograms on my shoulder

Don't cry out or beg for mercy

I will bend down to love

I am a drunken immortal hero

Don't say that crazy people are kind

Don't laugh because passion is hard to find

Don't be afraid to get drunk. Tomorrow is a another day

crazy and crazy and drunk while you are young

中 编

都市百态

Volume Ⅱ
Urban Forms

　　随着改革开放，中国都市题材影片迅速发展。此类题材影片展现了中国社会发展进程中的重要单元——城市化建设，它们见证了中国人民在经济和社会文化的快速发展进程中，个体生活发生的巨大改变。

　　在这一部分，我们选择了表现东北地区、中原地区和西南地区等几个具有代表性地域的电影作品。通过学习，学生可以了解中国城市的风貌特征和都市人群的生活图景。

With the reform and opening up, Chinese urban films have developed rapidly. This kind of films show an important element in the process of China's social development—urbanization. They have witnessed the great changes in the individual life of the Chinese people in the process of rapid economic, social and cultural development.

In this part, we have selected the film works that represent several representative regions such as the Northeast, the Central Plains and the Southwest. Through learning, students can understand the style and characteristics of Chinese cities and the life picture of urban people.

第四单元
钢的琴

📢 **本单元重点**

1. 了解电影《钢的琴》的艺术特色
2. 了解中国东北的基本知识

📢 **本单元难点**

1. 了解20世纪90年代中国下岗潮的背景
2. 分析电影《钢的琴》的隐喻和主题

Unit 4
The Piano in a Factory

 **Key points**

1. Learn about the artistic characteristics of *The Piano in a Factory*
2. Learn about the basic information on Northeast China

 **Difficult points**

1. Know about the layoff wave hit in China in the 1990s
2. Analyze metaphors and themes connoted in *The Piano in a Factory*

《钢的琴》：追忆美好时代

The Piano in a Factory：**Recalling the Beautiful Times**

一、丝路放映厅 Silk Road screen hall

导演：张猛

编剧：张猛

主演：王千源/秦海璐/张申英

类型：剧情/喜剧

制片国家/地区：中国内地

上映日期：2011 – 07 – 15

片长：119 分钟

英文名：*The Piano in a Factory*

Director：Zhang Meng

Screenwriter：Zhang Meng

Starring：Wang Qianyuan/Qin Hailu/Zhang Shenying

Type：Drama/Comedy

Production country/region：Chinese mainland

Release date：July 15，2011

Length：119 minutes

English name：*The Piano in a Factory*

主要获奖 Major awards

第 48 届台北金马影展：国际影评人费比西奖

第 23 届东京国际电影节：最佳男主角

第 14 届上海国际电影节：最佳影片、最佳导演

第 28 届中国电影金鸡奖：评委会特别奖、特别影片奖

The 48th Taipei Golden Horse Film Festival：International Film Critic Award（the FIPRESCI Prize）

The 23rd Tokyo International Film Festival：Best Actor

The 14th Shanghai International Film Festival：Best Film and Best Director

The 28th China Film Golden Rooster Award：Special Award of the Jury and Special Film Award

剧情梗概 Plot outline

在 20 世纪 90 年代的中国东北，下岗工人陈桂林（王千源饰）与女儿小元生活在一起，迫于生活，热爱音乐的陈桂林组成了一支业余乐队，在小镇上靠各类演出维生。妻子小菊（张申英饰）和卖假药的商人在一起，如今生活富裕，想回来和陈桂林离婚并带走女儿小元。陈桂林为了证明自己有能力抚养女儿，四处借钱为女儿买钢琴。小镇的工业已经没落，陈桂林的好友们大多已经下岗，生活拮据，买钢琴的钱无法凑齐。陈桂林和好友想出了去学校偷琴的办法，当场被警察逮捕。走投无路下，陈桂林有了一个大胆的想法，依靠一本俄国文献和钢铁厂留学苏联的老工程师指导，想为女儿手工打造一架钢琴。于是，他与女友淑娴（秦海璐饰）召集了昔日工友，在已经废弃的旧厂房里开始了造琴计划。与此同时，工厂里的两根标志性的大烟囱即将面临爆破拆除，工人们纷纷展开保卫烟囱的行动。

In Northeast China in the 1990s, the laid-off worker Chen Guilin（played by Wang Qianyuan）lived with his daughter Xiaoyuan. Forced by life, Chen Guilin, who loves music, formed an amateur band and made a living by doing various performances in the town. His wife Xiaoju（played by Zhang Shenying）got together with a businessman who sold fake drugs. She became rich and thought to come back to divorce with Chen Guilin and take her daughter Xiaoyuan. In order to prove his ability to bring up their daughter, Chen Guilin borrowed money everywhere to buy a piano for his daughter. The industry in the town had declined and most of Chen Guilin's friends were laid off. They were living in poverty and couldn't put together the money to buy a piano. Chen Guilin and his friends came up with an idea to steal a piano from the school. They were arrested by the police on the spot. Desperate，Chen Guilin had a bold idea. Relying on the Russian literature and the guidance of an old engineer from a steel factory that had studied in the Soviet Union，he wanted to build a piano for his daughter by himself. Thus，he and his girlfriend Shuxian（played by Qin Hailu）gathered some former workers and started the plan of making the piano in the abandoned old factory. At the same time，the two iconic chimneys in the factory were about to be demolished by blasting and workers took actions to defend the chimneys.

重要词汇 Important vocabularies

中国东北	zhōngguódōngběi	n.	Northeast China
业余	yèyú	adj.	amateur
离婚	lí//hūn	v.	divorce
借钱	jiè//qián	v.	borrow money
文献	wénxiàn	n.	literature
指导	zhǐdǎo	n.	guidance
保卫	bǎowèi	v.	defend

例句 Example sentences

1. 中国东北是一个很有趣的旅游目的地。

Northeast China is a very interesting tourist destination.

2. 作为一名业余选手，他的水平已经很不错了。

As an amateur player，his level is already very good.

3. 孩子的抚养权是这场离婚官司的焦点。

The custody of children is the focus of this divorce lawsuit.

4. 借钱的事情，我会认真考虑的。

I will seriously consider borrowing money.

5. 写论文的过程中，专业文献给了我很大帮助。

In the process of writing my thesis，professional literature has given me a great help.

6. 同学们在张老师的指导下排练新节目。

The students review the new program under the guidance of Mr. Zhang.

7. 保卫国家是每个人的义务。

It is everyone's duty to defend the country.

语言练习 Language practices

请为以下句子选择合适的词语进行填空。

Please fill in the blanks with the appropriate words for the following sentences.

1. 这场战役（   ）了领土的安全。

This battle served to （   ） the security of the territory.

2. 我的故乡在（   ）。

My hometown is in （   ）.

3. （   ）不还，会让你失去信用。

If you （   ） and you don't pay it back, you will lose your credit.

4. 结婚时开心，（   ）时伤心。

Happy when married and sad when （   ）.

5. 他利用（   ）时间学习了汉语。

He learnt Chinese by using the （   ） time.

6. 图书馆里有很多关于电影的（   ）。

There are many movies （   ） in the library.

7. 在妈妈的（   ）下，我学会了做菜。

With the （   ） of my mother, I learned to cook.

二、丝路大讲堂 Silk Road lecture hall

【导演特色】Featuring director

张猛，1975 年出生于中国东北。曾就读于中央戏剧学院舞台美术系，毕业于北京电影学院文学系，擅长舞美设计和剧本写作。电影《耳朵大有福》（2008 年）、《钢的琴》（2011 年）、《山上有棵圣诞树》（2012 年）等作品都由他自编自导。张猛导演的作品有非常精美的视觉设计，内容上多关注现实主义题材。在电影主题的表现上，张猛导演和世界著名的喜剧大师卓别林有点类似，善于将底层普通人的生活和心酸搬上银幕，特别是表现普通工人在艰苦的生活中乐观积极的生活态度，巧妙地将喜剧风格融入其中。

Zhang Meng was born in Northeast China in 1975. He studied in the Department of Stage Art of the Central Academy of Drama and graduated from the Department of Literature of

Beijing Film Academy. He excelled at play design and script writing. The films *Lucky Dog* (2008), *The Piano in a Factory* (2011), *The Christmas Tree on A Mountain* (2012) and other works were collected and directed by him. Director Zhang Meng's works have very exquisite visual design and pay more attention to realistic themes in content. In terms of the expression of the film theme, director Zhang Meng is similar to the world-famous comedy master Charlie Chaplin. His skill lies in bringing lit the sad drudgery of the powerless in society, and by juxtaposing it against their positive attitude displays the comedy of life.

【视觉风格】 Visual style

东北的冰天雪地和破落的工业小镇是影片的主要视觉场景。严峻的自然环境和影片的冷色调反映了工人们的生存境况。深色系的配色给人以压抑之感，作为影片的主色调，电影用灰色、棕色、蓝色构成了工业小镇破败萧条的景象。鲜明的红色起到了点缀作用。红色代表着热情和希望，淑娴和小云的红衣服，陈桂林的红色手风琴都是影片里温情的象征。横移镜头是本片的常见拍摄手法，开场时的横移长镜头可以交代环境和人物，扩展画面信息，片中几处横移长镜头制造了"画外惊喜"的喜剧效果。

The ice and snow in the northeast and the broken industrial town are the main visual scenes of the film. The severe natural environment and the cool color of the film reflect the living conditions of the workers. The dark colors give people a sense of depression. The film employs grays, browns and blue as its primary colors to evoke the atmosphere of the dilapidated and depressed industrial town. Bright red played a decorative role. Red represents passion and hope. The red clothes of Shuxian and Xiaoyun and the red accordion of Chen Guilin are all symbols of warmth in the film. A pan lens is a common shooting technique of this film. The pan long lens at the beginning introduces the environment and characters and expands the visual perspective. Several horizontal shift long lenses in the film create a comic effect of "surprise outside the picture".

【女性形象】 Female image

影片中刻画了两位女性人物形象，淑娴与陈桂林的妻子小菊，两者形成了鲜明的对比。小菊为了钱离家出走，离开陈桂林与卖假药的商人在一起。淑娴为了陈桂林，出钱出力帮助他完成造琴的梦想，去争夺陈桂林女儿的抚养权。淑娴是陈桂林可以一起组乐队的合作伙伴，也是他的知己和爱人。尽管本片是一个以男性角色为主导的电影，但淑娴这一角色展现了她独特的人格魅力——善良、重情义、敢爱敢恨。

The film depicts two female characters, Shuxian and Chen Guilin's wife Xiaoju, which form a sharp contrast. Xiaoju runs away from home for money and leaves Chen Guilin to be with a businessman selling fake drugs. For the sake of Chen Guilin, Shuxian pays money to help him complete his dream of making a piano and compete for the custody of Chen Guilin's daughter. Shuxian is Chen Guilin's partner who will form a band together with him. She is also his confidante and lover. Although this film is dominated by male characters, Shuxian's role shows her unique personality, her charm, kindness, respect for friendship, and daring to love and hate.

【喜剧风格】 Comedy style

喜剧是好莱坞乃至全球最受欢迎的电影类型之一。喜剧电影的特征是幽默化的语言和表演以及夸张的情节。一部优秀的喜剧电影除了引人发笑之外，还能引人深思，作为一种对时代或社会的批判手段使用。中国当代出现了许多优秀的现实主义题材喜剧电影，例如《疯狂的石头》（2006 年）、《落叶归根》（2007 年）、《人在囧途》（2010 年）、《无名之辈》（2018 年）等。它们和《钢的琴》一样，大多表现普通人的生活，展现当代中国人在逆境中自强不息的奋斗精神。

Comedy film is one of the most popular film types in Hollywood and worldwide. Comedy film is characterized by humorous language and performance, and exaggerated plot. An excellent comedy film can not only make people laugh, but also make people think deeply. It acts as a social commentary of the times. There are many excellent realistic comedy films in contemporary China, such as *Crazy Stone* (2006), *Getting Home* (2007), *Lost on Journey* (2010), *A Cool Fish* (2018), etc. Like *The Piano in a Factory*, most of them show the life of ordinary people and the struggling spirit of contemporary Chinese people to strive for self-improvement in adversity.

【多样化的配乐】 Diversified soundtrack

《钢的琴》中有多首配乐，符合 20 世纪 90 年代中国社会文化的多样性特征。在改革开放的时代背景下，西方文化和中国港台文化开始涌入中国大陆。因此，电影中的配乐主要有以下三类：

第一类是香港和台湾地区的流行音乐。80 年代末伊始，港台流行文化大量涌入中国大陆。除了服饰、餐饮等，流行歌曲也受到了广泛欢迎。电影中出现的《张三的歌》《心恋》都是广为传唱的流行歌曲。

第二类是中国的革命题材歌曲，影片中出现的《怀念战友》是中国著名电影《冰山上的来客》（1963 年）中的插曲，这首歌歌颂了战友之间的情谊。造琴就像陈桂林和工友们面临的一场战斗，《怀念战友》表现了陈桂林和工友们战斗般的决心。

第三类是具有异域风情的外国音乐。"超级马力欧兄弟"是日本任天堂公司开发并于 1985 年出品的著名游戏，在中国风靡一时。片中陈桂林为女儿制作纸质的琴键，"超级马力欧兄弟"游戏音乐响起，他的动作随着音乐的节拍进行剪辑，营造出游戏的轻松感。俄罗斯摇滚乐队 Lube 的一曲 "Skoro Dembel"，摇滚歌曲旋律激昂，节奏明快，与陈桂林团队的精神不谋而合。影片结尾，打扮成西班牙女郎的淑娴带领一群少女迈着舞步前进，陈桂林和他的乐队在一旁投入地演奏，《西班牙斗牛士之歌》将电影情绪推向高潮。

There are many soundtracks in *The Piano in a Factory*, which are in line with the diversity of Chinese society and culture in the 1990s. Under the background of reform and opening up, western culture and Chinese culture in Hong Kong and Taiwan began to flow into Chinese mainland. Thus, the soundtrack in the film mainly includes the following three categories:

The first category is pop music in Hong Kong and Taiwan. At the beginning of the late 1980s, Hong Kong and Taiwan pop culture poured into Chinese mainland. In addition to clothing, catering and so on, pop songs have also been widely welcomed. "Zhang San's Song" and "Love" in the film are popular songs widely sung.

The second category is China's revolutionary theme songs. The "Remembering the co-workers" in the film is an episode in the famous Chinese film *Visitors on the Icy Mountain* (1963). This song praises the friendship between co-workers. Making a piano is like a battle between Chen Guilin and his co-workers. "Remembering the co-workers" shows Chen Guilin's determination to fight with his co-workers.

The third category is foreign music with exotic customs. "Super Mario Bros." is a famous game developed by Nintendo and produced in 1985. It was all the rage in China. In the

film，Chen Guilin made paper keys for his daughter. The game music of "Super Mario Bros."
sounded. His actions were edited with the beat of the music to create a sense of ease in the
game. "Skoro Dembel"，a song by Russian rock band Lube，has a passionate melody and a
lively rhythm，which coincides with the spirit of Chen Guilin's team. At the end of the film，
Shuxian dressed as a Spanish girl，leads a group of girls to dance while Chen Guilin and his
band play enthusiastically. "The song of the Spanish Matador" pushes the mood of the film to
a climax.

【虚构舞台】 Fictional stage

《钢的琴》中的舞台分为现实和非现实的，虚构舞台的歌舞表演段落在片中多次出现，营造了主线故事之外的形式之美。偷琴被警察抓住的夜晚，出现了陈桂林在雪地里弹琴的场景，这是小人物的内心狂想。《钢的琴》中用来运送猪肉的货车、深夜的KTV包间、造琴的工厂都可以成为主人公们载歌载舞的舞台，既可以补充剧情，渲染情绪，又为影片增加了浪漫色彩。

The stage in *The Piano in a Factory* is divided into realistic and unrealistic. The song and
dance performance paragraphs of the fictional stage appear many times in the film，creating the
beauty of form outside the main story. On the night when the thief was caught by the police，
there was a scene of Chen Guilin playing the piano in the snow，which was the little man's
inner fantasy. The truck used to transport pork，the KTV private room at night and the piano
factory in *The Piano in a Factory* can all become the stage for the protagonists to sing and
dance，which not only supplements the plot，and evokes emotion，but also adds romance to
the film.

【烟囱的含义】 Meaning of chimney

20世纪90年代中期是中国下岗减员的高峰期，因为大量的国有企业经济效率低下，人员冗余。面对改革开放后私营企业和外资企业的冲击，国有企业不得不进行改革。其中一项就是辞退部分国有企业的职工，关闭亏损严重的企业。《钢的琴》中出现了两根烟囱，它们即将被爆破拆除。烟囱代表了中国大批国有企业和工人的命运，如果不进行生产力的革新，就要被时代淘汰。电影中的工人采取各种办法去阻止烟囱的爆破，实际上是对自己命运的抗争。

The mid-1990s was the peak of layoffs in China, because a large number of state-owned enterprises had low economic efficiency and redundant personnel. Facing the impact of the competition from private enterprises and foreign-funded enterprises after reform and opening up, the state-owned enterprises had to make reforms. One of them was to dismiss some employees of state-owned enterprises and shut down enterprises with serious losses. There are two chimneys in *The Piano in a Factory*, which are about to be demolished by blasting. Meanwhile, chimney hints the career prospect of mass state-owned enterprises and their employees. That is if there is no reform conducted to upgrade productivity, these enterprises shall be eliminated. The workers in the film take various measures to stop the explosion of the chimney, which is actually a struggle against their own fate.

【伟大的父亲】 Great father

影片主人公陈桂林下岗失业了，贫困使得妻子离开他，连他最爱的女儿小元都要离开他去大城市生活。他经历了用纸做琴—借钱未果—偷琴—造琴的一系列波折，最终仍失去了女儿的抚养权，但是他对女儿无私的爱感动了女儿和无数观众。在电影史中，也有很多著名的父亲角色，他们和陈桂林一样生活贫穷，但是都因为伟大的父爱活成了生活中的英雄。

The protagonist of the film, Chen Guilin, is laid off and unemployed. Poverty makes his wife leave him. Even his favorite daughter Xiaoyuan wants to leave him to live in a big city. He went through a series of twists and turns from making a piano with paper to borrowing money, stealing a piano and making a piano, and finally he lost the custody of his daughter. However, his selfless love for his daughter moved her and countless audiences. In the history of film, there are also many famous father figures. They live in poverty like Chen Guilin, but they have become heroes of life because of their great father's love.

【世界电影中那些伟大的父亲】 The great fathers in world films

（1）《寻子遇仙记》（1921 年）：导演卓别林，美国默片。本片是喜剧大师卓别林早期第一部长片电影（50 分钟）。片中由他扮演的主人公夏尔洛收养了一个弃婴，成为一位"父亲"，他不仅要摆脱警察的抓捕，还要防止小偷带走儿子。本片没有台词与声音，依靠卓别林出色的肢体语言完成演出，卓别林创造的"笑中带泪"的夏尔洛人物形象成为电影史上的经典。

（2）《偷自行车的人》（1948 年）：导演德·西卡，意大利新现实主义代表作品，本片对《钢的琴》的创作产生了极大的影响。《偷自行车的人》表现了第二次世界大战后意大利的社会状况，失业、贫困充斥社会。影片中的父亲好不容易找到了一份贴海报的工作，但是他倾其所有买的自行车被人偷走了，走投无路的父亲只能去偷别人的自行车，最终被警察抓走。

（3）《光猪六壮士》（1997 年）：导演彼得·卡坦纽，英国喜剧电影。北英格兰遭遇经济危机，重工业破败，钢厂工人大批失业。电影中的主人公盖兹（Gaz）就是一位父亲，他和其他五个下岗工人组成了一个表演脱衣舞的团体，演出赚钱，并最终获得了家人的支持和理解。大胆的创意和精湛的表演使本片成为英式幽默的典范。

（4）《当幸福来敲门》（2006 年）：导演加布里埃莱·穆奇诺，美国电影。主人公是一位落魄的父亲，妻子因为贫穷选择离开家。主人公只能与儿子相依为命，努力寻找工作。他们住过教堂的收容所，甚至住进了地铁的公共厕所。不管多么艰苦，父子俩始终相信幸福的生活一定会来临。有趣的是，影片中儿子的扮演者正是影星威尔·史密斯的儿子贾登·史密斯。

(1) *The Kid* (1921)：directed by Charlie Chaplin, is an American silent film. This film is the first feature film (50 minutes) of the early stage of comedian Chaplin. In the film, Charlotte, the protagonist he plays, adopts an abandoned baby and becomes a "father". He not only wants to escape being arrested by the police, but also prevents kidnappers from taking his son away. This film has no lines and voice, and relies on Chaplin's excellent body language to complete the performance. The Charlotte character image of "tears in laughter" created by Chaplin has become a classic in film history.

(2) *Bicycle Thieves* (1948)：directed by Vittorio De Sica, is a representative work of Italian neo-realism. This film had a great impact on the creation of *The Piano in a Factory*. *Bicycle Thieves* shows the social situation in Italy after the Second World War. Unemployment and poverty flooded their society. The father in the film managed to find a job hanging posters, but the bike he bought with all his money was stolen. The desperate father had to steal other people's bicycles and was finally caught by the police.

(3) *The Full Monty* (1997)：directed by Peter Cattaneo, is a British comedy film. Northern England suffered an economic crisis. Heavy industry collapsed and a large number of

steel workers lost their jobs. Gaz, the protagonist in the film, is a father. He and five other laid-off workers formed a group to perform stripteases, made money, and finally won the support and understanding of his family. Bold creativity and superb performance make this film a model of British humor.

(4) *The Pursuit of Happiness* (2006)：directed by Gabriele Muccino, is an American film. The protagonist is a poor father. His wife chooses to leave home because of poverty. The protagonist can only stick together with his son and try to find a job. They have lived in church shelters and even in public toilets on the subway. No matter how hard it is, father and son always believe that a happy life will come. Interestingly, the father and son in the film are actually father and son in real life, Will and Jaden Smith.

互动讨论 Interactive discussion

1. 结合剧情和老师的讲解，试着讲讲你对这几句话的理解。

Try to explain your understanding of these sentences in combination with the plot and the teacher's explanation.

（1）淑娴：别看钢厂和钢琴厂只差了一个字，可这差得老远去了！

Shuxian：Although there is only one word difference between the 钢厂 （gāng chǎng） steel factory and 钢琴厂 （gāngqín chǎng） piano factory, there is however a big difference！

（2）陈桂林：小菊回来了。她说要和我离婚，我同意了。她跟了一个卖假药的，她终于过上了梦寐以求的那种不劳而获的日子。

Chen Guilin：Xiaoju is back. She said she wants to divorce me and I agreed. She went off with a fake drug seller and she is finally living the kind of life she dreamed of, living a good life without working a day.

2. 回答以下问题，并进行讨论。

Answer the following questions and discuss them.

（1）"钢的琴" 在影片里有何象征意义？

What is the symbolic meaning of "The Piano in a Factory" in the film?

（2）在你的国家，有哪些伟大的父亲形象？试着举出一两个例子。

Are there any great role-models of fathers in your country? Try to give one or two examples.

三、延伸阅读 Extended reading

中国东北地区包括辽宁省、黑龙江省、吉林省（简称"东三省"）以及内蒙古自治区的东五盟市（呼伦贝尔市、通辽市、赤峰市、兴安盟、锡林郭勒盟），占地面积共计152万平方公里。

Northeast China covers an area of 1.52 million square kilometers, including Liaoning Province, Heilongjiang Province, Jilin Province (hereinafter referred to as the "Three Eastern Provinces") and the five Eastern League cities of Inner Mongolia Autonomous Region (Hulun Buir City, Tongliao City, Chifeng City, Xing'an League and Xilin Gol League).

农业 Agriculture

东北拥有丰富的农业资源，农业上从农林区、农耕区、半农半牧区过渡到纯牧区。东北地区森林覆盖率高，总蓄积量约占全国的三分之一，冰雪消融时间长，有助于发展农业及林业。东北是世界上除了乌克兰平原以及密西西比平原外，拥有肥沃黑土的平原地区，黑土肥力高，适合植物生长。再加上东北地区纬度高，寒暖分明，使得其粮食产量和质量均比较突出。吉林省、黑龙江省是中国的粮食大省。

Northeast China is rich in agricultural resources. It has transitioned from agricultural and forestry areas, agricultural and pastoral areas to pure pastoral areas. Northeast China has a high forest coverage, accounting for about one third of the total volume of the country. Ice and snow melt for a long time, which is conducive to the development of agriculture and forestry. Northeast China is a plain area with rich black soil in the world except for the Ukraine Plain and Mississippi Plain. The black soil has high fertility and is suitable for plant growth. Coupled with the high latitude and distinct cold and warm in Northeast China, its grain yield and quality are more prominent. Jilin Province and Heilongjiang Province are major grain provinces in China.

资源 Resources

东北地区拥有丰富的石油资源，已探明储量占中国的一半左右，拥有大庆油田（中国最大油田）、辽河油田和吉林油田三大油田。东北的煤炭、油页岩、石灰石资源也极其丰富。

Northeast China is rich in oil resources, with proven reserves accounting for about half of China's reserves. It has three major oilfields: Daqing Oilfield (China's largest oilfield), Liaohe Oilfield and Jilin Oilfield. Northeast China is also extremely rich in coal, oil shale and limestone resources.

工业 Industry

早在 20 世纪 30 年代，东北就已经建成完整的工业体系，成为东北亚最先进的工业基地。主要工业城市有沈阳市、大连市、鞍山市、抚顺市、吉林市、长春市、哈尔滨市等。东北地区一度占有中国 98% 的重工业份额，是全国的工业重镇。

As early as the 1930s, Northeast China had built a complete industrial system and become the most advanced industrial base in Northeast Asia. The main industrial cities include Shenyang, Dalian, Anshan, Fushun, Jilin, Changchun, Harbin, etc. Northeast China once produced 98% of China's heavy industry and was an important industrial region in China.

民族 Ethnic groups

中国东北主要的民族有汉族、满族、朝鲜族、赫哲族、鄂温克族、鄂伦春族等。由孙增田执导的纪录片《最后的山神》（1993 年）就记录了鄂伦春族人的生活习俗和宗教信仰。著名作家迟子建的小说《额尔古纳河右岸》获得第七届茅盾文学奖，用魔幻主义风格讲述了鄂温克人史诗般的故事。

The main ethnic groups in Northeast China are Han, Manchu, Korean, Hezhe, Ewenki, Oroqen, etc. The documentary *The Last Mountain God* (1993), directed by Sun Zengtian, records the living customs and religious beliefs of the Oroqen people. Chi Zijian's novel *The Right Bank of Erguna River* won the 7th Mao Dun Literature Award. It tells the epic story of Ewenki people in the style of magic.

饮食 Diet

东北地区的饮食被统称为北方菜，因为东北较为寒冷，所以其美食以大锅炖菜为主要做法，能够长期贮存的酸菜也成了寒冷东北的主要食材之一。锅包肉、大棒骨、东北乱炖、酸菜排骨、酸菜猪肉炖粉条、小鸡炖蘑菇等都是其特色菜品。

The diet in Northeast China is collectively referred to as northern cuisine. Because it is relatively cold in Northeast China, the main practice of its cuisine is pot stew. Sauerkraut, which can be stored for a long time, has also become one of the main ingredients in cold Northeast China. Steamed pork in pot, big stick bone, northeast random stew, pickled pork ribs, pickled pork stewed vermicelli, chicken stewed mushrooms and so on are all its specialties.

艺术 Art

东北的艺术种类多样，包括二人转、秧歌、剪纸、龙江剧等。其中，二人转最为著名。赵本山是中国家喻户晓的喜剧演员，曾在央视春节联欢晚会表演了《红高粱模特队》《昨天今天明天》《卖拐》《功夫》等多个优秀小品。2003 年，歌手雪村创作并演唱的一首歌曲《东北人都是活雷锋》走红全国，歌曲展现了东北人耿直、幽默的性格特点，结尾的一句"翠花，上酸菜"成为流行语。

There are various kinds of art in Northeast China, including Errenzhuan, Yangko, paper cutting, Longjiang Opera and so on. Among them, Errenzhuan is the most famous. Zhao Benshan is a well-known comedian in China. He once performed many excellent sketches such as *Red Sorghum Model Team*, *Yesterday*, *Today*, *Tomorrow*, *Abduction* and *Kung Fu* at the CCTV Spring Festival Gala. In 2003, a song written and sung by singer Xue Cun, "Northeast People are All Living Lei Feng", became popular all over the country. The song shows the upright and humorous characteristics of northeast people. The final sentence "Cuihua！Serve us sauerkraut" has become a popular phrase.

四、课后思考 After class thinking

1. 通过电影《钢的琴》和此节内容的学习，简述你对中国东北的印象。

Briefly describe your impression of Northeast China through the film *The Piano in a Factory* and the studying of this section.

2. 你认为下岗能给人带来什么样的影响？

What impact do you think layoffs can bring to people?

五、互动时间 Interaction time

学习歌曲《东北人都是活雷锋》，以角色扮演的形式将歌曲内容表演出来。

Learn the song "Northeast People are All Living Lei Feng" and perform the content of the song in the form of role play.

东北人都是活雷锋

词曲：雪村

演唱：雪村

老张开车去东北

撞了

肇事司机耍流氓

跑了

多亏一个东北人

送到医院缝五针

好了

老张请他吃顿饭

喝得少了他不干

他说

俺们那嘎都是东北人

俺们那嘎盛产高丽参

俺们那嘎猪肉炖粉条

俺们那嘎都是活雷锋

俺们那嘎没有这种人

撞了车哪能不救人

俺们那嘎山上有针蘑

那个人他不是东北人

台词：翠花！上酸菜！

Northeast People are All Living Lei Feng

Lyricist and composer: Xue Cun

Singer: Xue Cun

Lao Zhang drove to the northeast

Hit

The driver who caused the accident behave like a hoodlum

Run away

Thanks to a northeast man

Send to the hospital for five stitches

Okay

Lao Zhang invited him to dinner

He didn't do it when he drank less

He said

We Naga are from Northeast China

Our Naga is rich in Korean ginseng

Our Naga pork stewed vermicelli

Our Naga is all living Lei Feng

There is no such person in Naga

How can you not save people after hitting a car

There are needle mushrooms on our Naga Mountain

That man is not from Northeast China

Line: Cuihua! Serve us sauerkraut!

第五单元
火锅英雄

本单元重点

1.了解电影《火锅英雄》的人物关系
2.了解中国的火锅文化

本单元难点

1.分析电影《火锅英雄》的"英雄形象"
2.了解重庆作为影视作品取景地的原因

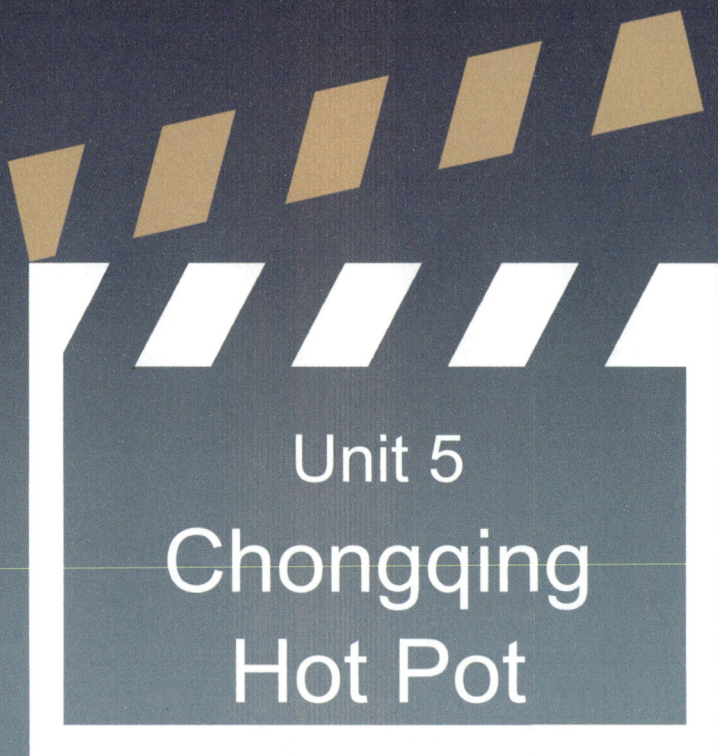

Unit 5
Chongqing Hot Pot

📣 Key points

1. Learn about the relationship between characters of *Chongqing Hot Pot*
2. Learn about the hot pot culture in China

📣 Difficult points

1. Analyze the "heroes" depicted in *Chongqing Hot Pot*
2. Know about the reason why Chongqing is highly valued by film directors

《火锅英雄》：沸腾人生的英雄

Chongqing Hot Pot：**The Hero of Boiling Life**

一、丝路放映厅 Silk Road screen hall

导演：杨庆

编剧：杨庆

主演：陈坤/白百何/秦昊/喻恩泰

类型：剧情/犯罪

制片国家/地区：中国内地

上映日期：2016－04－01（中国内地）

片长：98 分钟

英文名：*Chongqing Hot Pot*

Director：Yang Qing

Screenwriter：Yang Qing

Starring：Chen Kun/Bai Baihe/Qin Hao/Yu Entai

Type：Drama/Crime

Production country/region：Chinese mainland

Release date：April 1，2016（Chinese mainland）

Length：98 minutes

English name：*Chongqing Hot Pot*

剧情梗概 Plot synopsis

在布满防空洞的重庆，刘波（陈坤饰）、许东（秦昊饰）与王平川（喻恩泰饰）三个好兄弟合伙开着一家防空洞里的火锅店，名为"老同学洞子火锅"。由于经营不善，三兄弟准备把店转让。为了店铺能"卖个好价钱"，三人开始自行扩建，沿着洞子往里开挖，没想到意外凿开了隔壁银行的金库！濒临倒闭的火锅店和银行金库仅有"一洞之隔"，面对金钱诱惑的三人左右为难，特别是欠着赌债的刘波，生活基本走投无路。三人的初中女同学于小惠（白百合饰）恰巧在隔壁银行上班，三人计划，让刘波假装偶遇于小惠，请于小惠帮忙完成他们转移金库钱财的计划。另一边，一伙真正的劫匪预谋抢劫金库，因为这个"洞"，三兄弟勇敢拯救银行的人质，意外从生活的失败者成为英雄。

In Chongqing where bomb shelters are everywhere，Liu Bo（played by Chen Kun），Xu Dong（played by Qin Hao）and Wang Pingchuan（played by Yu Entai）run the hot pot restaurant called "the old mates hot pot restaurant". Yet，they want to transfer the restaurant to avoid further loss due to the poor revenues generated from it. To gain more income，they begin to dig a hole to enlarge their restaurant. Unexpectedly，they discover that the basement hole they have dug is separated by only a single wall from the bank vault next door，allowing them entrance to the bank vault from their restaurant，which is on the verge of collapse. Faced with the temptation of money，the three men are in dilemma，especially Liu Bo，who owes gambling debts. His life is basically at a loss. When they learn that Yu Xiaohui（played by Bai baihe），a former classmate from middle school is one of the bank employees，they determine to enlist her aid in deciding their future. As Liu Bo is won over to their views，they hear that a gang of robbers is busy robbing the bank vault and holding the bank staff，including Yu Xiaohui hostage. Liu Bo and his two best friends act without hesitation to rescue those trapped in the bank from danger. They are not losers but heroes.

重要词汇 Important vocabularies

防空洞	fángkōngdòng	*n.*	bomb shelter
火锅	huǒguō	*n.*	hot pot
转让	zhuǎnràng	*v.*	transfer
倒闭	dǎobì	*v.*	collapse
诱惑	yòuhuò	*n.*	temptation
英雄	yīngxióng	*n.*	hero

例句 Example sentences

1. 战争时期，防空洞起到了重要作用。

Bomb shelters played an important role during the war.

2. 嗨！晚上一起去吃火锅吧。

Hi! How about eating hot pot tonight?

3. 为了挽救公司，他决定转让股权。

He determines to transfer equities for supporting the company.

4. 谁也没有想到，这个商场也会倒闭。

It is a surprise to everyone that the mall is collapsed.

5. 敢于拒绝诱惑的人才是真正的自律。

A self-disciplined person is not allured by temptation.

6. 英雄难过美人关。

Even a hero shall fall into a beauty trap.

语言练习 Language practices

请为以下句子选择合适的词语进行填空。

Please fill in the blanks with the appropriate words for the following sentences.

1. 面对美食的（　　　　　），我实在难以拒绝。

I cannot resist the (　　　　) of tasty cuisine.

2. （　　　　　）是中国川渝地区的特色菜。

(　　　　) is the special cuisine in Sichuan-Chongqing area of China.

3. 每一个平凡人都有可能成为（　　　　）。

Everyone can be a (　　　　) someday.

4. 炮声一响，所有人都躲进了（　　　　）。

Hearing gunfire, everyone hides in (　　　　).

5. （　　　　）店铺的相关事宜已经谈妥。

The relevant matters related to (　　　　) the store have been negotiated.

6. 工厂大量（　　　　）带来的下岗潮不可避免。

It is inevitable that a large number of factories will (　　　　) and bring about a wave of layoffs.

二、丝路大讲堂 Silk Road lecture hall

【导演特色】 Featuring director

杨庆，1980 年生于中国重庆市，自编自导了《夜·店》（2009 年）、《火锅英雄》（2016 年）两部影片。杨庆擅长将喜剧片和犯罪片两种颇受欢迎的商业类型相结合，以繁华的都市为背景，讲述小人物的传奇经历。《夜·店》中的 24 小时便利店、《火锅英雄》中的洞子火锅店和银行金库都是封闭空间，作为故事的主要发生地，杨庆擅长在狭小的封闭空间中营造丰富的矛盾冲突和令人意想不到的故事走向，也能够设计出精彩的场面调度，使其作品深受年轻人的喜爱。

Yang Qing, born in Chongqing city in 1980, is the screenwriter and director of *One Night in Supermarket* （2009） and *Chongqing Hot Pot* （2016）. He excels at integrating comedy and crime elements, which are appealing in the film market, and crafting a legendary tale of ordinary people in a prosperous metropolis. As the main filming sites, the 24-hour convenience store in *One Night in Supermarket*, the cave hot pot restaurant and bank vault in *Chongqing Hot Pot* are all enclosed spaces. Yang Qing is able to juxtapose apparent contradictions in a narrow space with surprising endings, and to cast fabulous scenes as well. His films are popular among the youth.

【重庆方言】 Chongqing dialect

导演杨庆选择拥抱自己的故乡重庆，影片中主要人物使用的语言是重庆方言。方言使用强化了电影的地域特点，使故事和人物更为真实。重庆方言具有语调明快、风趣幽默的特点，特别是儿化音和语气词的频繁使用，使重庆话听起来更加随意、亲切。方言的使用建立了本片独特的幽默风格。电影中的劫匪四人组则使用普通话，从语言上鲜明地区分了人物的身份和阶级。

Director Yangqing made this film in his hometown Chongqing, and the main characters speak the Chongqing dialect, which strengthens the regional characteristics of the film and makes the plot and characters more realistic. The dialect features fast tones and changeable intonations, especially the frequent addition of r-ending retroflexion and discourse markers, thus it sounds informal and interesting, adding to the film's humorous appeal. With the four robbers speaking Putonghua, it aims to distinguish among differing identities and classes.

【犯罪片】Crime film

犯罪片是成功的商业类型片之一，产生于 20 世纪 20 年代的好莱坞。《火锅英雄》由一场紧张刺激的银行抢劫案开始，一伙戴着面具的劫匪闯进了重庆一家银行，直到他们在银行的金库内发现了一个洞。影片用倒叙的手法，从三兄弟开始转让火锅店重新讲起，直到最后再次回到抢劫案当天，劫匪与三兄弟的两条故事线相融合。生活中的普通人意外卷入了银行抢劫事件，和凶恶的劫匪展开了殊死搏斗，这样的犯罪故事使普通人蒙上了英雄的色彩。

Crime film is one of the successful genres of commercial film, firstly produced by Hollywood in the 1920s. In *Chongqing Hot Pot*, it portrays a crime activity enacted by robbers wearing masks. They go to one of the banks in Chongqing, and discover that they could exit via a subterranean hole. The film uses flashbacks, starting with the transfer of the hot pot restaurant by the three men, and finally returning to the day of the robbery. The two story lines of the robbers and the three men blend together. Undoubtedly, the story of ordinary people accidently caught up in a robbery and their righteous response, adds a sense of heroism, which is satisfying to viewers.

【洞子火锅】Cave hot pot

重庆是一座火锅的城市，也是一座布满防空洞的城市。在重庆，火锅店和防空洞一样密密麻麻，数量非常多，其中就有一些火锅店选择开在废弃的防空洞中。这也形成了重庆火锅的一道独特风景线。片中三位男主人公就在防空洞开了一家"老同学火锅店"，正是因为对它的扩建，才挖开银行金库。作为电影中的主要场景，不小心挖通金库、兄弟三人和于小惠商量事情、黑帮老大威胁刘波还钱却阴差阳错偶遇劫匪等重要情节都在此展开，洞子成了舞台化的展示空间。防空洞幽暗、局促，既是对三兄弟人生困境的写照，也是人与人之间阶级的隐喻。金库在地上，代表着财富，那里是属于上层人的空间。于小惠在银行也只能被"富二代"同事排挤。金库的正下方是人们维持生计的火锅店，正如刘波三兄弟不小心挖通金库是个"错误"一样，他们闯入了本不该属于他们的空间（阶级），这正是下层人无法逾越的空间壁垒。此外，洞子火锅店也为影片提供了独特的视觉造型，刻上了鲜明的重庆印记。

Chongqing is a city of hot pot, and also a city of bomb shelters. Hot pot restaurants and bomb shelters are all over the place in Chongqing. Some businessmen take a creative approach by trying to open hot pot restaurants in unused bomb shelters. The combination of these two elements creates something unique, just like "the old mates hot pot restaurant" run by three men in this film. If they hadn't attempted to enlarge the restaurant, they would not have dug a hole into the bank vault. As the main setting, "the old mates hot pot restaurant" witnesses a collision of incidents: a hole to enter the bank vault, negotiations between the three men and Yu Xiaohui, an accidental encounter between robbers and a crime boss who means to threaten Liu Bo for money. The dark and narrow space symbolizes the different dilemmas the three men encounter, and also functions as a metaphor of the class gap. The bank vault is located above ground where the upper class live in, and represents wealth. Even though Yu Xiaohui works there, she is isolated from her colleague born with a silver spoon. Just below the vault, there is the hot pot restaurant that the lower class wish to enlarge to make a living. The "error" made by the three men suggests that they tried to squeeze into the space (class) that is not meant for them, and consequentially the lower class is overwhelmed by the class barrier. Moreover, the cave hot pot restaurant arouses the audiences' attention and provides them with a unique perspective of Chongqing.

【石梯】Stairway

石梯依山势而建，是山城重庆独有的景观。石梯曲折蜿蜒，层次丰富，配合倾斜构图和运动镜头能够营造出节奏感。《火锅英雄》中刘波与劫匪的追逐就在石梯上完成，展现了两人漫长的追逐过程。这场追逐戏，利用暴雨的阴冷和泥泞，扩展了黑色的主色调，展现出重庆的市井建筑风格，凌乱拥挤的巷子和狭长的石梯配合着暴力打斗，共同再现了香港经典犯罪片中的视觉风格。

Stairways built along with the mountain is a unique landscape feature in Chongqing. The panoramic shot with the combination of dynamic tilted composition follows the meandering staircases, contributing to the sense of rhythm. In *Chongqing Hot Pot*, the extended chase scene between Liu Bo and robber is filmed on long stairways. Heavy rain and muddy stairways highlight the main color (black) that runs through the film, which not only convey the construction style of residential houses of Chongqing, but also suggest a typical Hong Kong crime film atmosphere, when they see a life and death struggle fought on the long staircases of narrow and messy lanes.

【长镜头】Long shot

长镜头是指用比较长的时间，对一个场景、一场戏进行连续的拍摄。长镜头的优点是能够比较完整地呈现连续性动作、还原空间。《火锅英雄》以快节奏的剪辑为主，长镜头并不多。但是影片中有一个独特的长镜头设计，即七哥手下和劫匪团伙在洞子火锅店内火拼的镜头，采用了横移长镜头，导演巧妙利用了洞子火锅店狭长局促的空间特点，在镜头的横移中，黑帮打斗的场面被慢镜头拉长、放大，美学意味十足，仿佛一幅逐渐铺展开的卷轴画，配合优美的弦乐，展现了"暴力美学"的风格。

A long shot is a camera shot that through the integrity of action, juxtaposes the settings and characters to portray their relationships with their surroundings and environment. *Chongqing Hot Pot* adopts fast-paced editing without too many long shots. Yet, a unique long shot is employed to present the conflict between followers of Qige and the robbers. Director Yang fully leverages the narrow but long cave hot pot restaurant scene, enlarging and expanding images by the addition of an eye-level full shot to depict a visual feast, "violence in art".

【一封情书】Love letter

于小惠写给刘波的情书一直被王平川收藏，因为王平川暗恋着于小惠。在信中，刘波是于小惠青春期爱慕的英雄。如今的刘波是一个一事无成的年轻人，欠下大笔赌债，和朋友合伙开的火锅店也面临转让。影片结尾，刘波冒着生命危险，对劫匪穷追不舍，却不是为了钱，而是为了劫匪背包中于小惠在学生时期给自己写的那封情书。于是，刘波再次成了于小惠心目中的那个英雄。《火锅英雄》就像是一封写给生活和人生本身的情书。

The love letter written by Yu Xiaohui to Liu Bo is kept by Wang Pingchuan, due to his unrequited love for her. She mentions in this letter that Liu Bo was a hero for her in her puberty. However, today the only thing striking about the young man, Liu Bo is a failed business combined with huge debts. The hot pot restaurant that he opened in partnership with his friends is also facing transfer. At the end of the film, Liu Bo puts his life at risk to chase a robber in hot pursuit, not for money, but for the letter that Yu Xiaohui wrote to Liu Bo when she was a student. For Yu Xiaohui, Liu Bo once again becomes a hero in her mind. *Chongqing Hot Pot* epitomizes a love letter to life and life itself.

【火锅情谊】Friendship of hot pot

刘波、许东、王平川三人在中学时就组成了"沙坪坝草蜢"组合，兄弟情谊维持了十多年。电影中有多次三人围坐在火锅前的场景，分别前要吃火锅，商量大事要吃火锅，火锅是一种情感的联系纽带，也是兄弟三人友情的见证。刘波潇洒冲动，王平川木讷诚实，许东精明圆滑，三个性格不同的人为了火锅店一度闹到分崩离析，一场银行劫案又让三兄弟再次团结。善良正直的于小惠在一顿火锅中决定加入兄弟三人的计划，和三兄弟建立了深厚的友情。

Liu Bo, Xu Dong and Wang Pingchuan formed a band called "Grasshoppers of Shapingba" in their middle school. They were sworn brothers for more than ten years. There are several scenes document in the film where they eat hot pot together, including the last meal for them or discuss important matters. Hot pot seems like a tie to connect them, and also witnesses to their friendship. Xu Dong is a man of sagacity. Liu Bo is an impetuous man but loyal to his friends. Wang Pingchuan is dull and honest. Despite these three different men having a bitter quarrel about the hot pot restaurant, the occurrence of the bank robbery unites them again. An upright and kind girl, Yu Xiaohui, decides to join the plan of the three men in a hot pot meal, and develops a deep friendship with them.

【反英雄】Atypical hero

《火锅英雄》的英雄并非传统意义上的英雄，和人们心目中对于英雄形象的认知大相径庭。首先是人物的反英雄化设定。三兄弟均有自己的缺陷，刘波嗜赌，打麻将欠下巨额赌债；许东则是生活中游手好闲的"妻管严"；王平川虽然勤劳踏实，但是生性懦弱。不完美的主人公们更接近我们生活中真实的市井小民形象，使人物塑造更具有说服力。其次是情节上的反英雄化。影片最后，刘波兄弟三人并没有靠着一腔热血战胜劫匪四人组，而是被劫匪绑在了火锅店内。最终的胜利，是依靠来收债的七哥和手下，在戏剧化的巧合中完成的。普通人的胜利和成功并不是依靠拼搏精神，而是阴差阳错的运气。黑色幽默中透出的是导演对于英雄神话的另一种"悲观"解读。

The hero in *Chongqing Hot Pot* is atypical and different from the perception of a hero in people's minds. Firstly, there is the atypical characters: all three men have their own shortcomings. Liu Bo is addicted to gambling, and burdened with great debts; Xu Dong is a henpecked man controlled by his wife and always keeps his hands into his pockets; Wang Pingchuan is diligent and reliable, but rather soft, even cowardly. These flawed characters are vivid and closer to the image of ordinary people in reality, which makes the film persuading. Secondly, the uncommon plots: at the end of the film, the three men boldly fight against robbers, but failed and are tied in the restaurant. Actually, the victory belongs to Qige and his followers, who mean to collect debts, but involve in the robbery in coincidence. It conveys that for an ordinary person, an unforeseen luck may contribute to success, not his efforts. It also functions as an unconventional "pessimistic" interpretation of the heroes' legend, delivered by the director with the addition of black humor.

互动讨论 Interactive discussion

结合剧情，谈谈你对以下台词的理解。

Combine the plot and try to show your opinions on the following lines.

1. 重庆的火锅店，比街上的出租车还多。

There are more hot pot restaurants in Chongqing than taxis on the street.

2. 胆大骑龙骑虎，胆小骑个老母鸡。

Heroes ride dragons and tigers. Cowards only ride old hens.

3. 情书中，于小惠写道："因为你不是一个失败者，你是我心中的英雄。"

In the love letter, Yu Xiaohui writes, "You are not a loser. You are my hero."

三、延伸阅读 Extended reading

1. 中国重庆 Chongqing, China

重庆，简称"渝"，别称"山城"，又称为"江城""火炉"。20 世纪末，重庆成为中国除北京、上海、天津外的四大直辖市之一，也是中国中西部唯一的直辖市。重庆东邻湖北、湖南，南边与贵州相邻，西边连接四川，北部紧挨陕西，占据着重要的地理位置。重庆作为新兴大都市，伴随着三峡移民工程，已经成为长江上游地区的经济、金融、科创、航运和商贸物流中心，成长为西南地区最大的工商业城市。经历过社会转型时期老工业基地改造后的重庆，也是中国重要的现代制造业基地。

Chongqing, referred to as "Yú" for short, is called "Mountain City", "Jiangcheng" or

"Huolu". Since the end of the 20th century, it is one of the four municipalities under the direct administration of the central government of the People's Republic of China (the other three are Beijing, Shanghai, and Tianjin). Chongqing serves as an important hub for its neighboring provinces, namely: Hubei and Hunan in the east, Guizhou in the south, Sichuan in the west, and Shaanxi to the north. As an emerging metropolis, along with the support of Sanxia Immigration Project, Chongqing has become the region's economic, financial, technology innovation, shipping, trade, and logistics center in the upper reaches of the Yangtze River, and has grown into the largest industrial and commercial city in the Southwest. Experienced the transformation of the old industrial base in the period of social transformation, Chongqing is also an important modern manufacturing base in China.

火锅文化 Hot pot culture

重庆是巴渝文化发祥地，重庆火锅位于重庆"十大文化符号"的榜首，起源于朝天门码头的火锅，带有浓厚的市井气息。重庆火锅具有非常悠久的历史和民众基础，在中国已经是一种非常大众化的烹饪方式，全国各地都能找到售卖重庆火锅的餐饮店。重庆火锅是中国传统饮食方式之一，起源于明末清初码头边的纤夫饮食。重庆火锅以牛油为底，麻辣鲜香为特色，涮食的主要原料有毛肚、猪黄喉、鸭肠、毛血旺、脑花等。与日本、西方国家的分餐制不同，吃火锅需要围坐在一起，在一口锅里分享食物。这种饮食方式无疑在潜移默化间拉近了人与人之间的距离，增加了人与人之间的接触和交流。无论男女老少，坐在火锅前均可平等参与和分享，无论荤菜素菜，下到火锅里皆是一样的美味。火锅的杂糅和包容性，代表着人际关系的认同、亲近。

Chongqing is the birthplace of Bayu culture. Hot pot here, a local dish, originates from the port of Chao Tian Men, ranking the top of "Chongqing's ten cultural icons". It has grown to be the most popular cuisine loved by the general public with an exceptionally long history. Therefore, in China, Chongqing hot pot restaurants have spread nationwide. It is recorded that Chongqing hot pot was one of the traditional Chinese foods first made by boat trackers working in ports in the transition from the late Ming Dynasty to the early Qing Dynasty. The spicy Chongqing hot pot base is mainly red chili oil, which is made with beef fat and different kinds of spices. People can add various kinds of food into the Chongqing hot pot, such as tripes, yellow larynx fillet, duck intestine, duck blood in chili sauce, and brain. Unlike dishes usually served on separate plates for individuals in Japan and western countries, people need to sit together and share food in a pot when eating hot pot. Undoubtedly, it brings people closer by giving them opportunities to communicate and interact. No matter gender or age, all people can enjoy hot pot equally. Meat or vegetables boiled in hot pot are all tasty. Hot pot embraces everything, which represents a closer and appreciative interpersonal relationship.

美食 Tasty food

　　重庆是中国有名的美食发源地之一，除了火锅，川渝菜系在中国也具有广泛的群众基础，是中国最受欢迎的菜系之一。川渝菜系的特点就是独特的麻辣口味，常见的重庆小吃有重庆小面、酸辣粉等。川渝菜系的代表菜有水煮鱼、回锅肉、酸菜鱼、辣子鸡、水煮肉片、鱼香肉丝、泡椒肥肠、粉蒸肉等。

Chongqing is one of the famous food birthplaces in China . In addition to hot pot, other dishes of Sichuan-Chongqing cuisine, which is one of the most popular cuisines in China, are also widespread and praised by many people. The cuisine features hot and spicy, such as Chongqing noodles, hot and sour rice noodles. Its representative dishes include boiled fish, twice-cooked pork, boiled fish with pickled cabbage and chili, chicken with chilies, boiled meats, Yu-shiang shredded pork, pig's intestines with pickled peppers, and steamed pork with rice flour.

雾都 The city of fog

　　重庆位于中国的西南部，被称为"雾都"。重庆的东南部被大巴山和武陵山两座大山阻隔，长江、嘉陵江等丰富的水资源使得空气湿度较高，空气中充斥着大量的水汽，难以散去，形成云雾天气。重庆的年平均雾日约为全年的三分之一，"雾都"因此得名。

Chongqing, located in the southwest of China, is known as the "Fog City". The southeast of Chongqing is separated by Daba Mountain and Wuling Mountain. The rich water resources of the Yangtze River and Jialing River make the air humidity high. The air is filled with a lot of water vapor, which is difficult to disperse, and forming a cloud weather. The annual average foggy days in Chongqing are about one third of the whole year, hence the name of "Fog City".

棒棒 Bang-bang

"棒棒"是一种职业，其实就是重庆的挑夫。他们的工具就是一米长的竹棒，因为重庆山城地形复杂，许多常规交通工具无法到达，因此诞生了"棒棒"这一独特的职业，他们用肩膀挑起竹棒帮客人送货，这些挑夫被重庆市民称为"棒棒军"。他们大多来自重庆周边农村，以自己的劳动力为生，很多影视作品中都有对这一职业的展现。

"Bang-bang" refers to itinerant porters in Chongqing. They use bamboo shoulder poles or bangzi to carry goods. In Chongqing's rough roads, many transportations are unavailable, thus the demand for brute human strength to haul loads induces more people to be bang-bang porters. They shoulder loads up and down steep hills here, and are known called as the "bang-bang army". Most of them are villagers from the steep hills around Chongqing who make a living using their stamina to carry loads in the city. Many films and televisions emerge these porters.

索道 Aerial cableway

重庆主城区有两条全国独一无二的跨江索道：嘉陵江索道（已拆除）、长江索道，最早建成于 1986 年，用于长江两岸的人员通勤，也是来重庆游玩必须体验的交通工具之一，许多影视作品里都出现过长江索道的身影。

There are two unique aerial cableways stretching across the Yangtze River in the main urban area of Chongqing city, including Jialing River Cableway (shut down) and Yangtze River Cableway. It was built in 1986 as a public transportation for commuting workers and as a sightseeing experience for tourists. This landmark has appeared in many television programs and films.

轨道交通 Rail transit

重庆依山而建，地势复杂，不但交通不便，修建地铁的难度也极大，因此重庆的城市轨道以轻轨为主。其中，单轨 2 号线的李子坝站因其"单轨列车穿楼而过"的奇景在网络上爆红，成为游客参观体验的地标景点。这是中国第一座与商住楼共建共存的轨道交通高架车站，于 2004 年 3 月建成。

Chongqing is built on the mountain with complex terrain. It is not only inconvenient to traffic, but also difficult to build a subway. Therefore, the urban rail in Chongqing is mainly light rail. Liziba, a monorail station on Line 2, is popular on social media for its spectacular depiction of "an apartment building that has been built with a train running through it". It is a favorite of tourists for its remarkable landscape. It serves as the first Chinese monorail station built with residential houses, which opened in March 2004.

长江大桥 Chongqing Yangtze River Bridge

重庆有着"桥都"的美誉，这与横跨在长江上的数十座大桥不无关系。夜幕中，长江大桥犹如光带，串联起山城南北，也划分着重庆的每一处老区和每一个新区，连接重庆作为一个大都市的过去与现在。

Chongqing has a reputation of "Bridge City", due to its more than 10 bridges across the Yangtze River. At night, Chongqing Yangtze River Bridge resembles a light belt, connecting the southern and northern parts, dividing the old and new districts, and binding the past and the present of Chongqing.

2. 影像重庆 Films produced in Chongqing

重庆一直都是电影导演的宠儿，山城的独特地貌和雾气弥漫的气候使重庆具有魔幻的特质。在重庆，可以看到复杂错落的建筑，轻轨甚至可以穿楼而过；在重庆，也可以看到历史与现在的交汇，古老与现代的碰撞；在重庆，还可以感受到浓烈的文化浸透，吃一口火锅，闯一番事业。重庆的山、重庆的水、重庆孕育的历史都极具地方特色，中国再也没有一个城市能够像重庆一样，一眼就能够清晰辨别。在重庆取景的中国电影有十几部之多。

（1）《周渔的火车》（2002 年）：由孙周导演。本片是一部经典爱情电影。这部电影的取景地就是在重庆，里面的火车站、过江索道，都能找到重庆的影子。雾蒙蒙的重庆，也让这个爱情故事更加浪漫和富有诗意。

（2）《日照重庆》（2010 年）：由王小帅导演。本片取材自发生在重庆的一起真实事件。长期漂泊在海上的船长林权海，因为忙于工作而忽略了家庭，他的儿子在超市抢劫伤人，被警方击毙。老父亲林权海踏上了返回重庆寻找真相的旅程。

（3）《长江图》（2016 年）：由王超导演。本片讲述了发生在长江上两个时空交错的魔幻爱情故事，展现了长江两岸的美景，倒叙的手法使故事显得扑朔迷离。

（4）《从你的全世界路过》（2016 年）：由张一白导演。本片用镜头将繁复的情感与重庆的夜色融合交织，"串烧"式的爱情故事也串联起解放碑、长江大桥等著名景点。

（5）《少年的你》（2019 年）：由曾国祥导演。本片是一部关注校园暴力的青春题材影片，女主角陈念遭到了魏莱等三个女同学的校园霸凌，小混混小北悄悄保护着她，甚至决定牺牲自己帮陈念顶罪。重庆长长的石梯，在片中成了魏莱失足致死的重要场景。

Chongqing is highly valued by film directors, for its unique geographical landscape and foggy climate, which makes Chongqing a secret metropolis. Here, buildings are in disorder, and an apartment building has been built with a train running through it. Here, this city follows the trend of modernization while keeping the essence of the old style. Here, a culture identity is prominent, that is to eat hot pot, and to be someone. Mountains, rivers and history in Chongqing have local characteristics. No other city in China can be clearly identified at a glance like Chongqing. More than 10 films have been shot in Chongqing.

（1） *Zhou Yu's Train* （2002）：it is a classic romantic movie directed by Sun Zhou. Filmed in Chongqing, it shows off the trains and the aerial cableway there. With the foggy climate, the romantic story is more poetic and stirring.

（2） *Chongqing Blues* （2010）：it is directed by Wang Xiaoshuai. It is an adaptation based on a true story. Lin Quanhai, a sea captain and father, is busy and seldom goes back home. One day, he is informed that his son has been shot by the police for robbery. In finding out what happened, he starts journeying back to Chongqing, and comes to realize that he knew little of his son.

（3） *Crosscurrent* （2016）：it is directed by Wang Chao. It tells a magic love story which happened in the two intertwined spaces on the Yangtze River. The surrounding scenery is included in this film. With the flashback method，the plot attracts audiences' attention.

（4）*I Belonged to You*（2016）：it is directed by Zhang Yibai. A camera documents the complex inner emotions reflected by the night scenery of Chongqing. Some highlight scenic spots，such as Chongqing Liberation Monument and Chongqing Yangtze River Bridge are shown successively among different love stories.

（5）*Better Days*（2019）：it is directed by Derek Tsang. It is a teen film with the theme of school bullying. The film is about the leading actress Chen Nian，who is viciously bullied by Wei Lai and her two friends while a teenage street thug Xiaobei determines to protect her silently and even to bear the blame for Chen Nian who is responsible for Wei Lai's accidental death. As an important filming place，the long stairway of Chongqing is the central focus of the accidental death of Wei Lai.

四、课后思考 After class thinking

1. 你喜欢吃火锅吗？你认为火锅文化的精髓是什么？

Do you like hot pot? What do you think about the essence of hot pot culture?

2. 谈谈你所在国家和地区的饮食文化有什么特点。

Talk about the characteristics of food culture in your region and country.

五、互动时间 Interaction time

一起来学习重庆方言吧。

Let's learn Chongqing dialect now.

做撒子：做什么 what are you doing

幺妹儿：年轻女子 young girl

千翻儿：爱捣乱、爱折腾 naughty

安逸：满意舒服 satisfied and comfortable

对头：好，没问题 no problem

要得：好的 okay

婆娘：老婆 wife

正南其北：说正经的 be serious

摆龙门阵：聊天 chat

扯谎俩白：撒谎不眨眼，不说真话 deception

第六单元
独自等待

本单元重点

1.了解电影《独自等待》的艺术特色
2.了解北京的城市地域风貌和民俗特征

本单元难点

1.分析剧中当代中国青年人的形象特征
2.了解改革开放政策下中国的城市化发展状况

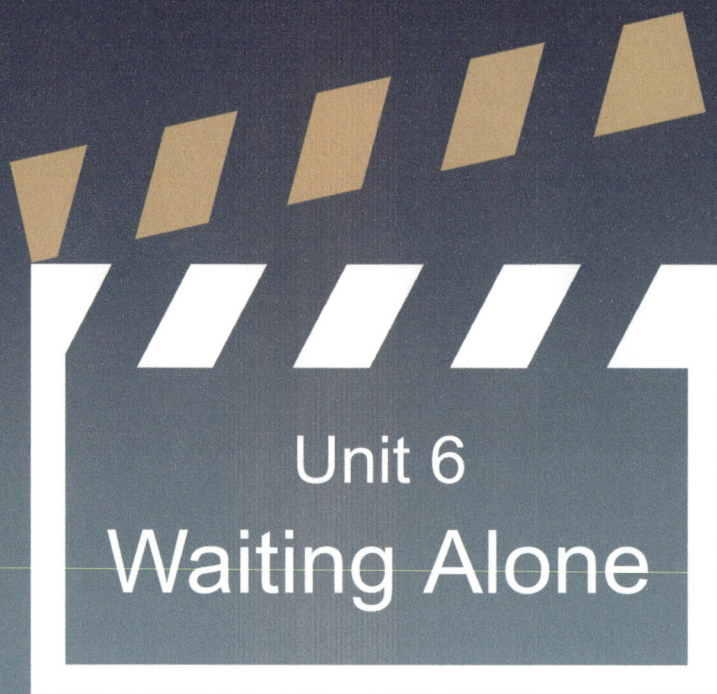

Unit 6
Waiting Alone

📢 Key points

1.Learn about the artistic characteristics of *Waiting Alone*
2.Learn about geological features and folk custom characteristics of Beijing

📢 Difficult points

1.Analyze the characteristics of the contemporary youth depicted in this film
2.Know about the development of urbanization in China with the support of the policy reform and opening up

《独自等待》：当代中国城市映像

Waiting Alone：Urban Images in Contemporary China

一、丝路放映厅 Silk Road screen hall

导演：伍仕贤

编剧：伍仕贤

主演：夏雨/李冰冰/龚蓓苾

类型：剧情/喜剧/爱情

制片国家/地区：中国大陆

上映日期：2005 – 09 – 08（中国大陆）/2004 – 10 – 26（东京电影节）

片长：107 分钟

英文名：*Waiting Alone*

Director：Dayyan Eng

Screenwriter：Dayyan Eng

Starring：Xia Yu/Li Bingbing/Gong Beibi

Type：Drama/Comedy/Romance

Production country/region：Chinese mainland

Release date：September 8，2005（Chinese mainland）/October 26，2004（Tokyo Film Festival）

Length：107 minutes

English name：*Waiting Alone*

主要获奖 Major awards

第 17 届东京国际电影节：亚洲之风/最佳亚洲电影（提名）——伍仕贤

第 25 届中国电影金鸡奖：最佳故事片（提名）——伍仕贤、最佳女主角（提名）——李冰冰、最佳美术（提名）——庄志良

第 9 届釜山国际电影节：新浪潮奖（提名）——伍仕贤

第 12 届北京大学生电影节：最佳男演员奖——夏雨、最佳处女作奖——伍仕贤

The 17th Tokyo International Film Festival：Asian Future Best Film Award—Dayyan Eng（nomination）

The 25th Golden Rooster Award for Chinese Film：Best Feature Film Award—Dayyan Eng（nomination），Best Actress Award—Li Bingbing（nomination），Best Art Direction Award—Zhuang Zhiliang（nomination）

The 9th Busan International Film Festival：New Currents Award—Dayyan Eng（nomination）

The 12th Beijing College Student Film Festival：Best Actor Award—Xia Yu，Best First Film Award—Dayyan Eng

剧情梗概 Plot synopsis

故事发生在改革开放后繁华的首都北京，主人公陈文（夏雨饰）刚毕业两年，是一名有抱负的作家，他与好友一起经营着一家古董店。在与好友们的一次聚会上，他邂逅了自己的梦中情人——刘荣（李冰冰饰）。在与刘荣两次简单的见面之后，好友们纷纷替陈文出谋划策，自此陈文对刘荣展开了猛烈的追求。刘荣对陈文忽冷忽热，陈文每日在期待和失望中等待和徘徊。一次偶然的机会，陈文发现自己竟是多年好友李静（龚蓓苾饰）的暗恋对象。好友们为了自己的梦想纷纷离去，陈文依旧经营着古董店，努力靠写作沉淀自我，也在平凡的生活中懂得了爱的深意。

Set in modern Beijing after the launch of reform and opening up, the leading actor Chen Wen (played by Xia Yu), who graduated from college two years ago, runs an antique shop with his friend and is an aspiring writer. At a party with his friends, he has just met his dreamboat Liu Rong (played by Li Bingbing) by chance. After two dates with Liu Rong, Chen Wen falls in love with her and is aided by his best friends as he tries his best to woo the dreamboat. However, Liu Rong seems to play cat and mouse with him, and Chen Wen suffers the disappointment of unrealized expectations every day. One day, Chen Wen suddenly recognizes that Li Jing (played by Gong Beibi), who is one of his best friends, crushes on him.　His friends leave to pursue their own dreams，while Chen Wen still operates the shop and continues to write，and gradually he learns about what true love is.

重点词汇 Important vocabularies

作家	zuòjiā	*n.*	writer
古董店	gǔdǒngdiàn	*n.*	antique shop
邂逅	xièhòu	*v.*	meet sb.　by chance
梦中情人	mèngzhōngqíngrén	*n.*	dreamboat
梦想	mèngxiǎng	*n.*	dream

例句 Example sentences

1. 我想成为一名有创作才能的青年作家。

I wish to be a talented young writer.

2. 周日的古董店是收藏家的淘物乐园。

On Sunday，the antique shop is just like a vault for collectors.

3. 和她在公交车上邂逅，我感到喜出望外。

Such a surprise for me to meet her by chance.

4. 我的梦中情人有着一头乌黑的长发。

My dreamboat has long black hair.

5. 只要努力，我们的梦想并不遥远。

As long as we are working hard，we should realize our dreams.

语言练习 Language practices

请为以下句子选择合适的词语进行填空。

Please fill in the blanks with the appropriate words for the following sentences.

1. 她与他偶然（　　　　）于街角的咖啡店，这便是他们爱情故事的开端。

She （　　　）at a coffee bar in the street corner, then their love story started.

2. （　　　）享有充分的创作自由。

A （　　　）desires the extreme freedom to write what he likes.

3. 两人决定把宝珠卖给（　　　）。

Two men determine to sell jewelry to （　　　）.

4. 今天我梦到了我的（　　　）。

Today，I dream my（　　　）.

5. 他的（　　　）是在广阔的蓝天上飞翔。

His（　　　）is to fly in the vast blue sky.

二、丝路大讲堂 Silk Road lecture hall

【导演特色】 Featuring director

伍仕贤，美籍华人导演，中国电影导演协会会员。主要代表作有《东二十二条》（1997 年）、《车四十四》（2001 年）、《独自等待》（2005 年）、《形影不离》（2012 年）、《反转人生》（2017 年）。伍仕贤的电影以其独特的叙事视角对现今社会的变化发展进行了精准捕捉，他的作品关注社会中的普通人群，通过还原生活的本来面貌，反映社会现实，从而引发观众的思考。同时，发挥喜剧语言的独特魅力也是其作品的一个突出特征。

Dayyan Eng is a Chinese American filmmaker and a member of China Film Director's Guild. The well-known films directed by him include *East 22nd Street*（1997），*Bus 44*（2001），*Waiting Alone*（2005），*Inseparable*（2012），and *Wished*（2017）. He employs a unique narrative perspective of focusing on grassroots in the community to faithfully reflect the change and development of current society. His films focus on the common people in the society and reflect the social reality by restoring the original appearance of life，thereby provoking the audiences' thinking. Meanwhile，employing comedy language，one of the prominent features in his films，makes it more appealing.

【第一人称】 First person narrative

第一人称叙事是电影叙事手法的一种，它为影片增加了主观色彩。这部影片以主人公陈文轻松幽默的语言贯穿故事始终，采用第一人称的讲述方式，夹杂主人公的内心独白，加强了影片的真实性和幽默感。影片中的第一人称视角让影片讲述的故事更加清晰明了，引起观众的共鸣。陈文似乎游走于观众（观看者）与角色（被看者）之间，使得观众的代入感极强。影片清新、幽默的整体气质让整个观影过程不会枯燥乏味，观众的情绪随着影片的节奏而变化。

A first person narrative is a mode of storytelling in films, which allows the audience to see the mind's eye view of the narrator. In *Waiting Alone*, a first person protagonist Chen Wen narrates the story in a relaxed and humorous tone, and his accompanying inner monologue, which enables an objective, light-hearted approach. Moreover, the storyline of this film told by Chen Wen is more likely to be understood and resonate with audiences. As the plot unfolds, it seems that Chen Wen could almost be one of the audiences rather than a character in the film. The fresh and humorous atmosphere far from boring the audience, attracts them, and leads them through a series of mood changes as the plot develops.

【都市青春】 Urban youth

和21世纪之后大多数国产青春片不同，影片《独自等待》中的青春成长主线虽围绕着主人公的爱情故事线索展开，但重点放置于人物的内心成长和对外部世界的探索上，以一种新鲜的、充满希望的积极态度，呈现出中国城市化建设背景下年轻人的精神面貌。

Unlike most teen films produced in the 21st century, *Waiting Alone*, though follows the protagonist's love story, focuses more on the characters' psychological growth and their explorations of the external world with a fresh and hopeful positive attitude, aiming to present a youthful spirit amid the Chinese urbanization.

【名字的"秘密"】 "Secrets" behind characters' names

影片中的三个主要人物建构看似简单，却糅合了导演对于人物性格、命运的暗示。爱好写作、经营着一家古董店的普通文艺青年陈文，其名字中的"文"即表明他的文学梦，同时透露出他的单纯和简单。夏雨的演绎则给人物增添了北京人独有的慵懒而潇洒的气质。梦想着成为大明星的三流演员刘荣，其名字中的"荣"则表现了她对于名与利的渴望，她执着于追求物质上的富足，却牺牲了个人精神层面的需求。表面疯癫、充满男孩子气的李静，其名字中的"静"暗示了她心底流淌着的含蓄细腻，懂得爱情规则的"进与退"。影片中每个人的爱情虽没有大篇幅的细节展示，却以一种全景式的图景描绘着都市男女们不同的生活状态、情感方式，引起观众的共鸣。

The storyline of the three leading characters is not difficult to understand. However, the connotations behind their names refer to their different characteristics and destinies. Chen Wen, an ordinary young adult running an antique shop, who loves to write fiction, has the first name character "Wen" meaning that he aspires to be a writer, and that his inner characteristics reflect innocence and frankness. Star Xia Yu makes this character true to life, providing audiences with a real image of the unrestrained and frank Beijing people. Liu Rong, a nameless actress, who eagerly wants to be a well-known star, has the first name character "Rong" suggesting that she seeks fame and fortune rather than mental improvement. Li Jing is an energetic tomboy, her first name character "Jing" hints that she is a sensitive girl and has a sense of propriety in terms of a romantic relationship. The film does not describe their love stories in detail, but presents different living conditions and romantic attitudes among different urban youth, which strongly resonates with audiences.

【自然光线】Natural light

光线是影像构成的重要元素，影片中导演运用大量的自然光线，向观众展现了北京这座城市的本来面貌，凸显了一群怀揣梦想、充满青春朝气的年轻人。自然光线的使用客观地呈现了陈文生活的弧线，增强了故事的真实性和人物的亲和力。

Natural light is an essential factor in cinematography. The use of abundant natural light in this film allows audiences to see a true picture of Beijing where a group of energetic youths strive to achieve their dreams. It also faithfully presents the life of Chen Wen, which enhances the truth of the story and the friendly image of the characters.

【流行音乐】Pop music

声音元素的设计能够加强人物内心状态的外向化表现，配合影片情绪和剧情的发展而变化。影片中流行音乐的使用，营造出浓厚的都市氛围和现代青春气息。影片中配乐《超级巨星》欢快的节奏配以刘荣的出场，惊艳了观众和主人公陈文的内心，浓郁的爱情味道和浪漫的氛围在陈文的内心散开，预示着陈文梦中情人的出现。这段音乐再次响起时伴随着陈文爱情的破灭，无数甜蜜的画面闪现在其脑海里，陈文此刻内心的失望和苦闷与之前的浪漫形成强烈的对比。

Characterization can be suggested through music motifs. As the plot continues, the film score shifts to suggest the mood or spirit of the film. In the film, pop music creates an atmosphere full of the youthful energy of a modern city. The pop music "Super Star", one of the film scores, is played when Liu Rong appears and catches audiences' and Chen Wen's eyes. From first sight, Chen Wen falls in love with Liu Rong and believes that Liu Rong is his dream boat. Yet, the song is played again when Chen Wen fails to woo Liu Rong, while countless memories occur in his head repeatedly. Unlike the flipped romance when they first met, he feels disappointed and upset at that moment.

【都市影像】 Urban image

影片故事的发生地设置在北京，影片还原了北京都市青年快节奏的生活方式，男女约会的场所、服装、道具充满着时代感和现代感。咖啡厅、台球厅、KTV、迪厅等现代都市男女生活的标志性地点，引发了都市青年强烈的认同感。当时流行的 Zippo 打火机、Nokia 手机深度还原了那个时代的流行趋势，切合了都市青年的审美心理。演员、古董店老板、吉他手、录音师等充满现代感、青春感的流行职业通过影像表现出来，导演成功把握了都市青年的生活语境和充满朝气的现代生活状态。

Set in Beijing, the film faithfully documents the fast-pace lives of young adults. Sites where they date, costumes they wear and props all showcase prominent modernization. For example, cafes, billiard rooms, KTV and night clubs, in which males and females socialize with each other, identity with urban youth. Besides, the trendy Zippo lighters and Nokia phones indicate the fashion at that time and are popularized among the youthful majority. In terms of their jobs, including actress, antique shop owner, guitarist and sound engineer, these emerging careers pursued by young people through the lens draw a real picture of the environment in which urban youth live out their positive lifestyles.

互动讨论 Interactive discussion

1. 你认为影片的喜剧元素体现在哪些方面？

Where and how do you think the comedy elements have been implied?

2. 说说你对"陈文"这一人物形象的理解。

Discuss your opinions of the character "Chen Wen".

三、延伸阅读 Extended reading

人们对于一座城市的记忆往往来源于建筑、历史或生活，北京的城市记忆不仅来自崎岖窄小的胡同、气势恢宏的故宫，而且也建立于新时代以来北京高速发展的城市面貌。北京有着浓厚的文化底蕴、悠久的历史内涵、丰富的艺术元素，成为许多影视作品的故事发生地和取景地，众多以"北京"为背景的影视作品纷纷出现在大众的视野，《找乐》《民警故事》《夏日暖洋洋》《四世同堂》《北京爱情故事》等影视剧呈现出浓郁的京味儿，将北京的地域特征、文化特色和民俗风情相融合，深入地刻画和展现出北京人独有的大大咧咧、豪爽洒脱、包容、爱面子等性格特征。

（1）《城南旧事》（1983 年）：本片根据林海音的同名短篇小说改编，讲述的是 20 世纪 20 年代末，小女孩英子随父母从台湾来到北京，在城南胡同度过的一段童年时光。影片渲染了人物身上所透露的中国人固有的善良品质和吃苦耐劳的精神。

（2）《北京，你早》（1990 年）：20 世纪 90 年代的北京，人人浮躁。早早迎接这个城市的曙光的除了环卫工人，还有公交司机和售票员，影片讲述的就是他们之间的青春和爱情。现在在北京乘坐公交是游览这个城市最便宜的手段，而老北京人怀恋的是以前三角钱一趟的公交车。

（3）《洗澡》（1999 年）：由于改革开放政策的实施，在 20 世纪 90 年代的北京，大片大片的胡同被拆迁，许多胡同居民的生活因此被迫改变，影片记录的就是某胡同拆迁前的最后时光，以及北京特有的"洗澡文化"。导演张杨用镜头记录着京城记忆，那种狭窄而又充满尘土气息的胡同，有着车铃铛声与老北京话交织的胡同，绝非现在青砖大瓦、充满游客不见居民的胡同，因为那是充满人间烟火气息的老北京胡同。

Generally speaking, the architecture, history and lifestyle of a city alway leave people with a deep impression. When people come to Beijing, they are not only impressed by its narrow and rugged hutongs and the magnificent Palace Museum, but by its modern appearance in a new era. Embodied with profound cultural connotations, a time-honored history, and rich forms of art, Beijing is well known for being a setting in literature and a location in many movies and television shows, such as *Looking for Fun*, *On the Beat*, *I Love Beijing*, *Four Generations Under One Roof*, and *Beijing Love Story*. All these allow audiences to see a vivid Beijing where Beijing citizens are casual, straightforward and forthright, tolerant, and concerned about their reputations, by integrating regional and cultural features and folk customs.

（1）*My Memories of Old Beijing*（1983）：the film is adapted from the short fiction of the same name written by Lin Haiyin. Set in the late 1920s, a little girl Yingzi moves to Beijing from Taiwan with her parents. During her childhood they live in a hutong in the southern part of the city. The inherent goodness and resilience of Chinese people seen in the characters are given a colored account in this film.

（2）*Good Morning，Beijing*（1990）：set in the 1990s, people are in hot pursuit of a better life. In addition to sanitation workers, the bus drivers and conductors also greet the early dawn of the city. The film is about a love story between a young driver and young conductor. Today, taking buses is the cheapest way to visit Beijing, while in the past, a one-way ticket in Beijing cost only 0.3 yuan.

（3）*Shower*（1999）：since the launching of reform and opening up policy, many Beijing hutongs were demolished in the 1990s and residents had to change their lifestyles. The film presents the unique "shower culture" in Beijing before the demolition of a hutong. Director Zhang Yang shows the city, where people lived in narrow and bustling hutongs, filled with tinkling bicycle bells and the Beijing dialect. Unlike splendid hutongs full of crowds of tourists with fewer residents, old hutongs are attached to daily life.

北京冬奥会 Beijing Winter Olympic Games

北京是第一个举办夏季奥林匹克运动会和冬季奥林匹克运动会以及亚洲运动会三项国际赛事的城市，也是继1952年挪威的奥斯陆后时隔70年第二个举办冬奥会的首都城市，这是中国历史上第一次举办冬季奥运会。

Beijing is the first city in the world to have hosted three international sport events, including the summer and winter editions of the Olympic Games and Asian Games. It is also the second capital city, following Norway's Oslo to host the Winter Olympic Games after 70 years, since 1952. For China, it was the first time to host the Winter Olympic Games.

北京国际电影节 Beijing International Film Festival

北京国际电影节创办于2011年，是在国家电影局指导下，由北京市人民政府、中央广播电视总台主办的大型国际电影活动。电影节以"共享资源，共赢未来"为活动主旨，旨在汇聚世界电影优秀成果，增进国际电影交流合作，推动跨区域、跨文化的电影传播，实现电影人和电影资本的跨文化合作，拓展国产电影国际传播空间，推动中国电影"走出去"，是北京市建设世界城市、打造东方影视之都的重点文化活动。

　　北京国际电影节在每年4月中旬举办，为期8天左右，其间影片竞赛、电影展映、市场会展等同时进行。天坛奖是电影节的最高奖项，以"天人合一，美美与共"为核心价值理念，旨在发现全球最新佳作，鼓励电影多样性。第十一届北京国际电影节于2021年9月21日至9月29日举办，开闭幕影片分别为《长津湖》《兰心大剧院》。

Founded in 2011, Beijing International Film Festival (BJIFF) is supported and sponsored by the China Film Administration, China Media Group and Beijing Government. Themed as "In Pursuit of a Shared Dream", the festival is an important cultural activity for bolstering Beijing one of the global cities and the Chinese capital of films and television. It aims to provide a high-profile forum for the interaction between the Chinese and the international film industries to share marvelous movies, to enhance their communication and cooperation with each other, and to promote cross-regional and cross-cultural film popularization. It purposes to achieve intercultural cooperation of filmmakers and capitals, popularize domestic films to the international community and fuel the "go out" of Chinese films.

The Beijing International Film Festival is kicked off in the middle of April every year, lasting about 8 days. Within that periods, film competitions, film exhibitions and market exhibitions are run in parallel. The Tiantan Award is the top prize of the BJIFF. Its aim is to discover and present recent outstanding films from across the globe, and to encourage diversity in cinema. The 11th BJIFF was held from September 21 to September 29, 2021. The opening and closing ceremony films are *The Battle at Lake Changjin* and *Saturday Fiction*.

北京胡同 Beijing hutongs

　　北京胡同是久远历史的产物，它反映了北京历史的面貌，有着丰富的内容。北京的胡同绝不仅仅是城市的脉络、交通的衢道，更是北京普通老百姓生活的场所，京城历史文化发展演化的重要舞台。它记下了历史的变迁、时代的风貌，蕴含着浓郁的文化气息，好像一座民俗风情的博物馆，烙下了人们各种社会生活的印记。从一个个大大小小的四合院中可以了解北京市民的生活，包括他们的生活方式、生活情趣和邻里关系。

　　北京胡同的形成是随着北京城的形成而变化、发展演进的。大约在五十万年前，这块地界开始有了原始人居住，不过那时只是住在天然洞穴里而已。到了距今一万到四五千年间，这里出现了原始氏族公社，开始住上了简易房屋。北京十大胡同分别是南锣鼓巷、烟袋斜街、帽儿胡同、国子监街、琉璃厂、金鱼胡同、东交民巷、西交民巷、菊儿胡同和八大胡同。

It is said that the real culture of Beijing lies in hutongs. They act as a time capsule and depicting the historical and cultural development of Beijing. Hutongs of Beijing are more than just traffic lanes; they are also people's homes. Hutongs represent an important cultural element of the city of Beijing. It records the changes of history, the style of the times, and contains a strong cultural atmosphere. It functions as a museum to make a heavy imprint on their inhabitant's social lives, and helps to preserve original and authentic customs and habits of old Beijing, which enables people to learn about their lifestyles, cultural tastes and neighboring ties when visiting Siheyuan.

The history of Beijing hutongs can be traced back to more than 500,000 years when cavemen inhabited the area and lived in the natural caves. From ten thousand to four or five thousand years ago, primitive clan communal societies settled here, and built simple houses. Today, ten popular Beijing hutongs are Nanluogu Lane, Yandaixie Street, Mao'er Hutong, Guozijian Street, Liulichang Cultural Street, Jinyu Hutong, Dongjiaomin Lane, Xijiaomin Lane, Ju'er Hutong and Bada Hutong.

北京庙会 Beijing temple fair

　　北京庙会是中国传统民俗文化活动，庙会又称"庙市"或"节场"。这些名称可以说正是庙会形成过程中所留下的历史"轨迹"。一种社会风俗的形成有其深刻的社会原因和历史原因，而庙会风俗则与佛教寺院以及道教庙观的宗教活动有着密切的关系，同时它又是伴随着民间信仰活动而发展、完善和普及起来的。现在的庙会还有许多不同于旧庙会的地方，比如吃，豆汁等京味儿小吃依然保留，同时增加了很多年轻人喜欢的各地小吃；比如人，以前是老人带着孩子来逛庙会，现在逛庙会成了年轻人游玩的时尚；比如演出，以前表演的都是北京花会，主要是踩高跷、戏曲演出等，形式比较单一，现在全国各地的演出单位齐聚北京庙会，表演节目丰富多彩。北京的春节庙会已经不仅仅是礼佛拜神之地，节日里人们以庙会为中心，朋友相聚、全家同游、同事相随，增进感情。

Beijing temple fair is a traditional Chinese folk cultural activity, which is also called "Miao Shi" or "Jie Chang". These names can be said to be the historical "track" left by the formation of the temple fair. The formation of a social custom has its profound social and historical reasons, while the custom of temple fairs is closely related to the religious activities of Buddhist temples and Taoist temples. At the same time, it is developed, improved and popularized along with the folk belief activities. Differences are reflected in several aspects. Firstly, various kinds of local snacks like Douzhi (fermented green bean juice) are available, as well as other popular snacks favored by young people. Secondly, participants (or celebrants) are mostly the elderly accompanied by their grandchildren. Now, it is touted by young people as a kind of fashion activity. Thirdly, a diversity of activities such as the flower fair, stilts and opera offer an enriching experience. At present, the Beijing temple fair held in the Spring Festival is not just a sacrificial ceremony, but a venue for fostering good relationships among friends, families and colleagues.

四、课后思考 After class thinking

1. 在你的国家有没有以名胜古迹而闻名的古城？介绍给大家。

In your country, are there any ancient cities that are places of interest? Show us.

2. 谈谈你最喜欢的北京美食，并描述一下它的味道和形状。

Talk about your favorite food of Beijing and describe their taste and shape in detail.

五、互动时间 Interaction time

学习演唱片中的流行歌曲"Super Star"，注意感情要充沛哦！

Let's sing the pop song "Super Star" together, please be vigorous!

Super Star

演唱者：S. H. E

填词：施人诚

笑　就歌颂　一皱眉头就心痛

我没空理会我　只感受你的感受

你要往哪走　把我灵魂也带走

它为你着了魔　留着有什么用

你是电　你是光　你是唯一的神话

我只爱你　You are my super star

你主宰　我崇拜　没有更好的办法

只能爱你　You are my super star

手　不是手　是温柔的宇宙

我这颗小星球　就在你手中转动

请看见我　让我有梦可以做

我为你发了疯　你必须奖励我

你是电　你是光　你是唯一的神话

我只爱你　You are my super star

你主宰　我崇拜　没有更好的办法

只能爱你　You are my super star

你是　意义　是天是地是神的旨意

除了　爱你　没有真理

火　你是火　是我飞蛾的尽头

没想过要逃脱　为什么我要逃脱

谢谢你给我　一段快乐的梦游

如果我忘了我　请帮忙记得我

你是电　你是光　你是唯一的神话

我只爱你　You are my super star

你主宰　我崇拜　没有更好的办法

只能爱你　You are my super star

你是电　你是光　你是唯一的神话

我只爱你　You are my super star

你主宰　我崇拜　没有更好的办法

只能爱你　You are my super star

You're my super star boy

Super Star

Singers：S. H. E

Lyricist：Derek Shih

Your laughter merits my praise，your frown hurts my heart

I have no time for myself，only have attention for you

Where are you going? You had my soul with you

My soul is obsessed with you，no good to keep it anyway

You are thunder，you are light，you are the only legend

I only love you，You are my super star

You will rule，I will obey，there is no better way

I can only love you，You are my super star

Your hands are not hands，it's the tender universe

I'm just the little planet that travels in it

Please，notice me，so I could live in my fantasy

I'm addicted to you，you have to reward me

You are thunder，you are light，you are the only legend

I only love you，You are my super star

You will rule，I will obey，there is no better way

I can only love you，You are my super star

You are the meaning

you are heaven，Earth，and God's order

There is no other truth than loving you

Fire，you are the fire，you are the end of me—the butterfly

Never thought of running away，why should I

Thanks for giving me such a beautiful dream

If I forget myself, please help to remind me

You are thunder, you are light, you are the only legend

I only love you, You are my super star

You will rule, I will obey, there is no better way

I can only love you, You are my super star

You are thunder, you are light, you are the only legend

I only love you, You are my super star

You will rule, I will obey, there is no better way

I can only love you, You are my superstar

You're my super star boy

第七单元
甲方乙方

📢 **本单元重点**

1.了解电影《甲方乙方》的喜剧手法
2.了解中国北京的基本情况

📢 **本单元难点**

1.了解电影《甲方乙方》中反映的社会现象
2.了解北京作为中国首都的重要地位

Unit 7
The Dream Factory

📢 **Key points**

1.Learn about the comedy techniques employed in *The Dream Factory*
2.Learn about the basic information on Beijing, China

📢 **Difficult points**

1.Know about social phenomena revealed in *The Dream Factory*
2.Know about the important role of Beijing as the capital city of China

《甲方乙方》：好梦一日游

The Dream Factory：Your Dream Come True Today

一、丝路放映厅 Silk Road screen hall

导演：冯小刚

编剧：冯小刚/王刚

主演：葛优/刘蓓/何冰/冯小刚/英达

类型：喜剧

制片国家/地区：中国大陆

上映日期：1997 – 12 – 24

片长：87 分钟

英文名：*The Dream Factory*

Director：Feng Xiaogang

Screenwriter：Feng Xiaogang/Wang Gang

Starring：Ge You/Liu Bei/He Bing/Feng Xiaogang/Ying Da

Type：Comedy

Production country/region：Chinese mainland

Release date：December 24，1997

Length：87 minutes

English name：*The Dream Factory*

主要获奖 Major awards

第 21 届大众电影百花奖；最佳故事片、最佳男演员——葛优、最佳女演员——刘蓓

The 21st Hundred Flowers Award：Best Feature Film Award，Best Actor Award—Ge You，Best Actress—Liu Bei

剧情梗概 Plot synopsis

在北京，有四个善良、热情的年轻人成立了一个"好梦一日游"公司，帮助人们实现自己的梦想。试营业的时候，引来了一批突发奇想的顾客。这些人中，有想要当大将军的书商，有想要当英雄的厨师，有想要体验贫穷生活的富豪，有想要体验平常人生活的女明星，有想要获得真爱的年轻人，有想要体验"受气"的普通市民，还有一个工程师想要和罹患癌症的妻子在北京团圆。姚远（葛优饰）、周北雁（刘蓓饰）、钱康（冯小刚饰）、梁子（何冰饰）四个年轻人扮演着各种角色帮客人们圆梦，用他们的真情、真心使他人的人生圆满。姚远把和周北雁结婚的房子借给了工程师夫妇，周北雁也因为姚远的正直决定嫁给他……

In Beijing, a "Your Dream Come True Today" company to help people realize their dreams virtually, was established by four kind-hearted young adults. At the company's soft-opening, there were some unusual requests by customers. Among them, a bookstore owner dreams to be a general; a chef wishes to be a hero; a rich man wants to live poor life; a female star is eager to disappear from the public's view; a youth desires to find true love; a civilian yearns to be bullied; an engineer yearns for a reunion in Beijing with his wife who has been diagnosed as with advanced cancer. They four, Yao Yuan (played by Ge You), Zhou Beiyan (played by Liu Bei), Qian Kang (played by Feng Xiaogang), Liang Zi (played by He Bing) play various roles who wholeheartedly help customers not only fulfill their dreams but also provide them with a full life. Yao Yuan lends the marriage house for marrying Zhou Beiyan to the engineer and his wife, which touches Zhou Beiyan so deeply, she decides to marry him because of his integrity.

重点词汇 Important vocabularies

善良	shànliáng	*adj.*	kind-hearted
厨师	chúshī	*n.*	chef
工程师	gōngchéngshī	*n.*	engineer
角色	juésè	*n.*	role

| 人生 | rénshēng | *n.* | life |
| 正直 | zhèngzhí | *adj.* | integrity |

例句 Example sentences

1. 善良的人总是乐于助人。

A kind-hearted people always wants to help others.

2. 我们的饭店需要招聘一名厨师。

We need to hire a chef.

3. 老师是人类灵魂的工程师。

Teachers are the engineers of the human soul.

4. 扮演好每一个角色，是演员的职责。

It is the responsibility of each actor to play a role well.

5. 人生的路需要走好每一步。

Every step should go well in a person's life.

6. 正直的人永远不畏惧邪恶。

A man of integrity is never afraid of evil.

语言练习 Language practices

请为以下句子选择合适的词语进行填空。

Please fill in the blanks with the appropriate words for the following sentences.

1. 我这次演的（　　　　）是一名医生。

The （　　　　） I played this time is a doctor.

2. （　　　　）掌握着大桥修建的进度。

An （　　　　） is responsible for the progress of bridge construction.

3. （　　　　）就像大海，难免起起伏伏。

（　　　　） is an undulating sea, and people have to deal with ups and downs.

4. 他是一个如此（　　　　）的老师，以至于他深受学生和家长的爱戴。

He is such a （　　　　） teacher to students and their parents admire him very much.

5. 在中国，（　　　　）的薪资很不错。

（　　　　） in China earn（s） a good salary.

6. 他为人（　　　　），敢仗义执言。

He is a man of （　　　　）, speaking out for justice.

二、丝路大讲堂 Silk Road lecture hall

【导演特色】 Featuring director

冯小刚，1958 年 3 月出生于中国北京，是中国内地著名的导演、编剧及演员。1989 年之前，冯小刚曾在多部影视作品中担任美术师。1991 年，由冯小刚编剧的中国首部情景喜剧《编辑部的故事》令其声名大噪，之后他又执导了《北京人在纽约》等电视剧。1994 年，冯小刚开始独立执导电影，《甲方乙方》（1997 年）、《不见不散》（1998 年）、《没完没了》（1999 年）等 20 世纪 90 年代经典都市题材喜剧电影，奠定了冯小刚中国"最卖座"导演的地位。2000 年后，冯小刚的创作开始走向多元化，他导演了犯罪片《天下无贼》（2004 年）、古装动作片《夜宴》（2006 年）、战争电影《集结号》（2007 年）、灾难片《唐山大地震》（2010 年）、历史剧情片《一九四二》（2012 年）等，并通过电影《老炮儿》（2015 年）中的精彩表演获得最佳男演员奖。冯小刚被称为中国"贺岁片之父"，其作品最大限度地把商业性与艺术性相结合，他擅长使用类型片框架，不仅不排斥商业广告，还坚持明星策略，注重营销宣传，获得了良好的票房效果。冯小刚的作品还特别关注市民阶层的喜怒哀乐，对都市生活进行了幽默化的展现，用温情的态度消解生活中的磨难。

Feng Xiaogang, born in Beijing on March 1958, is a prominent director, screenwriter and actor. Prior to 1989, he served as an art designer in many films and television shows. In 1991, Feng Xiaogang shot to fame as the screenwriter of the first Chinese sitcom, *Stories from the Editorial Board*. After that, he directed several television shows, like *A Native of Beijing in New York*. Since 1994, he has directed films independently. Some urban comedy blockbusters produced by him in 1990s, include *The Dream Factory* (1997), *Be There or Be Square* (1998), *Sorry Baby* (1999), which established his position as the most successful director in China. After 2000, he directed diverse genres of films, such as the crime film, *A World Without Thieves* (2004), the costume action film, *The Banquet* (2006), the war film, *Assembly* (2007), the Chinese disaster-drama film, *Aftershock* (2010) and the Chinese historical film, *Back to 1942* (2012), etc. Moreover, he won Best Actor Award for a brilliant performance in *Mr. Six* (2015). Feng Xiaogang established himself in a Chinese genre called "Father of New Year's celebration films". He adds abundant aesthetic elements to various types of commercial films. He is an expert in establishing the framework of film genres, adopting the strategy of entertainers' great viewership rather than excluding commercial advertisements, and focuses on marketing, which has resulted in a huge box office success. Feng Xiaogang's films also pay special attention to the joys and sorrows of the public class, and show a humorous expression of urban life, and resolve the hardships of life with a warm attitude.

【贺岁片】New Year's celebration films

《甲方乙方》于 1997 年上映以后，以 400 万元的成本获得了 3 600 万元的票房，获得当年国产电影票房冠军。《甲方乙方》是中国第一部瞄准新年特定档期创作的商业电影，并且采用了导演分成的模式，成为中国内地第一部真正意义上的贺岁片。冯小刚之后的《不见不散》《没完没了》等喜剧电影也都是采用类似模式、针对新年档期制作的贺岁片。由于中国的农历新年——春节大致在每年的 2 月，现在的"贺岁档"已经从之前的每年 12 月到次年 1 月扩展为每年的 11 月底到次年的 3 月初。其间涵盖了圣诞节、元旦、春节、情人节等多个节日，片方也会集中为此档期制作并投放高质量、大制作的电影，这些影片被称为"贺岁片"。

The Dream Factory (1997) grossed 36 million yuan at the box office with production costs of 4 million yuan, ranking first in domestic box office revenues in 1997. It was the first New Year's celebration film released in Chinese mainland in a Chinese Lunar New Year, and employs the method to distribute box office revenues to film directors, debuting Feng's success in television dramas. He has adopted similar methods to produce and release other films in New Year's celebration films season, such as *Be There or Be Square* and *Sorry Baby*. Initially, the New Year's celebration films season in China was exclusive to the films which were debuted close to the Chinese Spring Festival, and screened from December of the previous year to the end of January of the following year, covering almost a one-month-long period of time. Now, the period has been extended, lasting nearly three months from the end of November to early March of the next year. That is to say, audiences can view numerous high-quality films on Christmas Day, New Year's holidays, Chinese Lunar New Year holidays and Valentine's Day, spanning the New Year's celebration films season.

【游戏情境】 Role-playing game setting

四个自由职业的青年创办了"好梦一日游"公司，通过给予特定的情境和人物角色扮演帮助顾客圆梦。公司会设定好游戏化的夸张情境，主人公通过扮演角色达到体验人生的目的。在游戏机制的保护下，体验人并不会真正地受到伤害，比如"英雄梦"里遭受的严刑拷打并不会真的受伤。这种设定让影片巧妙地连接了真实生活和虚构、幻想，幽默的情节并不完全脱离生活，反而有了一定的合理性。"好梦一日游"公司演员们夸张的表演和顾客们体验游戏情境时的糗态百出成为本片喜剧效果的重要元素。

A "Your Dream Come True Today" company founded by four freelancers provides customers with immersive role-playing to help fulfill their dreams. The company designed a virtual game setting ahead of schedule and allows customers to experience what they desire by role playing. With the guidance of game protection mechanisms, participants can't actually be injured. For example, the one who desired to be a hero is not harmed by suffering rough torture. Surprisingly, the setting establishes a bridge between real life and virtual vision and illusion, which makes the comedy plots acceptable. On top of this, extravagant performances by the four, and funny reactions by the participants are key comedy elements to provoking spontaneous outbursts of laughter from audiences.

【段落叙事】 Paragraph narration

在本片中，六个故事成为独立的段落，通过"好梦一日游"公司串联起来，导演冯小刚用独特的叙事方式将不同主题的故事和人物自然地融合在一起，每个小故事都有自己的起承转合。在保持每个段落独立的完整叙事和不同主题的同时，影片保持在一个主线之中，完成传统线性叙事中的开端—发展—高潮—结尾。影片中，当姚远决定把他结婚用的房子借给工程师，圆他和重病的妻子在北京的"团圆梦"的时候，影片达到了故事的高潮。作为工作人员的姚远已经将"梦"带进了现实，或者说通过自己的生活帮他人圆了梦。

It's composed of 6 separate parts, which are linked by "Your Dream Come True Today" company. Director Feng adopts a unique narration to tell stories of different characters harmoniously, while each of them has a distinctive plot setting. Telling separate parts with various topics, the film keeps the main storyline and follows the traditional way in which the story unfolds，embracing four elements，beginning，development，climax，and denouement. The story that a house lent by Yao Yuan to the engineer for a reunion in Beijing with his wife suffering from a serious disease happens when the film reaches the climax of the story. Yao Yuan，an employee of the company，has sacrificed his own creature comforts to help customers fulfill their dreams as much as possible.

【语言幽默】 Verbal humor

冯小刚的喜剧电影并不像卓别林的喜剧，依靠滑稽的动作引人发笑，也不像周星驰的经典喜剧电影创造许多天马行空的故事，用陌生化的效果营造喜剧情境。《甲方乙方》中，机智幽默且生活化的台词成为冯小刚市民喜剧电影的主要特色。《甲方乙方》的剧本改编自王朔的小说《你不是一个俗人》，本片汲取了小说中的语言特色，带有"京味儿"的经典台词让日常生活中带着痞性的自嘲、调侃成为人物的银幕话语。影片的开场是姚远的独白："我叫姚远，现年 38 岁，未婚。人品四六开，优点六，缺点四，是个没戏演的演员。1997 年的夏天，我和在家闲着的副导演兼我的女友周北雁、道具员梁子、编剧钱康，合伙填补了一项服务行业的空白，名曰：好梦一日游。"带有自嘲的语言，真诚的语气，能够快速地把观众带入故事氛围之中。当钱康接到已经饿得生吃活鸡的富豪时，对富豪说："一切都会好起来的，是吧，等再过两年，山里头也富了，你要再想吃苦受罪，就得往沙漠无人区送你了。"既调侃了富豪，也传达出中国经济发展、农村逐步富裕的美好愿景。

Unlike the comedy style of Charlie Chaplin which adds pathos to humor，or Stephen Chow who excels at adding unique nonsensical stories to comedy films，Feng Xiaogang prefers to adopt humorous and plain lines，which is a prominent feature in his films. The language style of *The Dream Factory*，adapted from *You Are not a Layman* written by Wang Shuo，is carried in the words full of Beijing flavor，which shortens the distance between actors and audiences. *The Dream Factory* starts with the monologue delivered by Yao Yuan，in a mocking but sincere tone. "My name is Yao Yuan，a 38-year-old unmarried man，not a very kind but a good one. After all，my strengths surpass my shortcomings. In the summer of 1997，unemployed vice director and my girlfriend Zhou Beiyan，propman Liang Zi，screenwriter Qian Kang and me unveiled a revolutionary service，called 'Your Dream Come True Today'." Hearing that，audiences couldn't wait to see the plot development. When Qian Kang receives the rich man who has been starved to eat live chicken, he says to the rich man, "Everything will be alright, right? After several years, people in remote mountain areas shall live a prosperous life. If you want to endure hardship again, I have to send you to the desert areas." The words not only satires the rich, but also conveys the vision that China's economic development has achieved impressive results and the life condition in rural areas has been continuously improved.

【戏仿】 Parody

"戏仿"指的是对于经典文本的模仿和解构,在影视作品里主要体现在对经典电影片段的模仿,达到致敬或者消解原文本内涵的作用。作为喜剧电影经典手法的戏仿,更偏向于解构的艺术效果,通过对经典文本的再演绎打破观众的既定印象和心理期待,营造出人意料的喜剧效果。《甲方乙方》中想要当大将军的书商的故事段落,主要戏仿了好莱坞经典电影《巴顿将军》(1970 年),但是战争片中的严肃性和紧张感因为各种意外情况被消解,取而代之的是与战争氛围格格不入的滑稽效果。另一个例子是"受气梦"的故事里,姚远和周北雁仿照了电影《白毛女》(1951 年)中地主的造型,以扮丑的造型和尖细的声音说出台词"地主家也没有余粮啊",这已经成为中国电影中的经典喜剧场景。

"Parody" refers to a literary or musical work in which the style of an author or work is closely imitated or deconstructed for comic effect or in ridicule. When it comes to films and television shows, parody is more likely an imitation of a specific target or subject for paying tribute to classics or deconstruction which is highlighted in comedy films. Based on classics, parody reinterprets plots, providing audiences novel and unexpected contents and creating a surprising comic effect. For instance, "Dream to be a general", one of the stories in the film *The Dream Factory*, adopts a parody based on *Patton* (1970), a classic Hollywood cinema. Funny interpretation mitigates the serious and urgent appeal delivered by this war film and adds to the film's humorous appeal. In another story "Dream to be bullied", Yao Yuan and Zhou Beiyan imitate a landlord couple portrayed in the film *The White-haired Girl* (1951). Both of them dress up to be ugly, and Yao Yuan says in a mean tone, "Even a landlord does not have extra food to spare", adding to the film's comedy and satire effect.

【好梦一日游】Your Dream Come True Today

"好梦一日游"是本片中帮顾客实现梦想的公司，由赋闲在家的演员姚远和同样从事影视工作的伙伴创办。影片中他们共接待了七位顾客，这七个梦点缀了普通人平凡的生活。

（1）"将军梦"：图书店的老板沉迷于巴顿将军的传记，于是找到"好梦一日游"公司，希望当一天巴顿将军。由于巴顿将军太过凶残，经常命令枪毙手下，姚远提前结束了体验。图书店的老板被姚远教育："好好卖书，当你的良民，国家由咱强大的人民解放军保卫着。"

（2）"英雄梦"：爱传秘密的厨师想要当一天守口如瓶的英雄，保守住秘密。姚远告诉厨师，秘密就是："打死我也不说。"当遇到美人计、严刑逼供时，厨师都轻易交出了秘密，没想到大家都误会了他真的是"打死也不说"的英雄。

（3）"受气梦"：男人觉得妻子对自己百依百顺，肯定是因为受气是一件享受的事情，于是要求过受气的一天。在地主家干了一天苦力，遭受了一天不公正待遇以后，他终于体会到妻子的不易。

（4）"恋爱梦"：年轻人因为恋爱屡屡受挫而想不开，想要自杀，居委会大妈求助"好梦一日游"公司。周北雁假扮阿拉伯公主，精心准备了一场浪漫的约会，给年轻人以希望。

（5）"吃苦梦"：富豪尤万成想要体验吃苦的生活，姚远将他送回了自己的老家。没想到，当姚远来接富豪的时候，富豪早已饿得"眼冒绿光"，吃光了村子里的鸡。走时富豪承诺投资一个养鸡场，提高村民的生活质量。

（6）"平凡梦"：女明星唐丽君受不了明星的繁忙生活，想要远离演艺圈，过普通人的生活。姚远和周北雁为女明星开了新闻发布会，宣布唐丽君正式退出演艺圈。当回普通人的唐丽君受不了没人关注的落寞日子，身边的工作人员也都离她而去。她只能打电话央求姚远，能不能再让她红回去。

（7）"团圆梦"：姚远与周北雁在医院遇到了正在哭泣的工程师，他在北京奋斗多年，却依旧住在集体宿舍，长期和妻子分居两地，工程师的妻子已身患癌症，时日无多。姚远和周北雁一致决定把房子借给工程师，让他能和妻子在北京圆一个"团圆梦"，妻子最终在幸福中离去了。

"Your Dream Come True Today" company is established to fulfill customers' dreams by unemployed actor Yao Yuan and his partners working in the film industry as well. In the film, they supply services for seven customers, which bring them unusual but satisfying experiences.

(1) "Dream to be a general": for losing himself in reading a biography of General George S. Patton, the bookstore owner asks the "Your Dream Come True Today" company for help to be the general for one day. In a dream setting, because of his cruelty in shooting his followers freely, Yao Yuan quits prematurely. At the end of the experience, the owner is criticized by Yao Yuan. He says, "Run your bookstore cheerfully, and be a man observing disciplines and law. Our country is safeguarded by the powerful People's Liberation Army."

(2) "Dream to be a hero": a blabbermouth chef wishes to be the hero who can keep secrets unwaveringly for one day. Yao Yuan says, "I won't talk even if I am going to die", and requires the chef to keep it. Facing a beauty trap and rough torture, the chef does not resist but speaks out easily. However, the three partners misunderstand that he is a "hero" who won't talk even if he is going to die.

(3) "Dream to be bullied": a husband believes that his wife obeys him in everything because being bullied brings her joy. So, he requires to be bullied as a tenant for one day. While, doing continuous coolie labor, he feels too aggrieved to tolerate it. He finally recognizes that his wife is treated unfairly.

(4) "Dream to find true love": a young adult wants to commit suicide for he has always been dumped in relationships. An elder worker of a residents' committee hopes "Your Dream Come True Today" company will cheer him up. Zhou Beiyan pretends to be an Arab princess who falls in love with the young man, which raises his hopes to live.

(5) "Dream to live poverty": a wealthy man You Wancheng wants to experience living in poverty, and Yao Yuan sends him to his hometown, a poor village. Unexpectedly, the man is starving and has eaten all the chickens across the village. Before he leaves, he promises to open a poultry farm for improving the villagers' standard of living.

(6) "Dream to be an ordinary person": a female star Tang Lijun is troubled by extravagant attention (from the public) notice. She eagerly wants to escape public attention and live as a normal person. For that, Yao Yuan and Zhou Beiyan host a press briefing to announce Tang Lijun is retiring from public life with immediate effect. After experiencing a normal life, Tang Lijun aspires to be noticed again. Meanwhile, all her means of making a living have disappeared. She has to beg Yao Yuan to help her shoot to fame again.

(7) "Dream to reunite": Yao Yuan and Zhou Beiyan see a crying man at a hospital.

Upon enquiring they learn that he is an engineer, who has strived to live a better life in Beijing for many years. But he still lives in a dormitory and has had to be apart from his wife for a long time. Unfortunately, his wife now has an advanced cancer and her days are numbered. Yao Yuan and Zhou Beiyan unanimously decide to lend their house to the engineer, so that he and his wife could have a "reunion dream" in Beijing. The wife finally departs in happiness.

互动讨论 Interactive discussion

1. 结合剧情和老师的讲解，试着讲讲你对这几句话的理解。

Combining the plot with the teacher's explanation, try to talk about your understanding of the following sentences.

（1）姚远：我们这不搞三六九等，凡是群众需要的就是我们乐意奉送的。

Yao Yuan: We treat people equally. Whatever people require is what we are happy to give.

（2）尤老板（富豪）：拉倒吧你，我都想一辈子和龙虾睡一块儿了！

Boss You (wealthy man): No way! I prefer to sleep with lobsters!

2. 回答以下问题，并进行讨论。

Answer the following questions and have a discussion.

（1）《甲方乙方》里面的七个小故事，你最喜欢哪一个？为什么？

The Dream Factory is composed of seven stories. Which one is your favorite? Why?

（2）如果你能有机会参加"好梦一日游"，你要实现什么样的梦想？

If you have an opportunity to experience the service supplied by "Your Dream Come True Today" company, what dream do you want to realize?

三、延伸阅读 Extended reading

北京，史称"燕京""北平"，是中国的首都、直辖市、国家中心城市，也是整个中国的政治中心、文化中心、国际交往中心、科技创新中心。北京总面积为 16 410 平方千米，截至 2020 年底，北京市常住人口为 21 893 095 人，占全国人口的 1.55%，现有东城、西城、海淀、朝阳、丰台、昌平、大兴、怀柔、平谷等十六个辖区。

Beijing, historically known as "Yanjing" and "Peking", is the capital of China, as well as one of municipalities and national central cities. It is also the nation's political, cultural center and China's most important center for international interactions and technological innovations. The city covers an area of 16,410 square kilometers and has a permanent population of 21,893,095 people by the end of 2020, which accounts for 1.55% of the national gross population. It is divided into 16 districts, namely Dongcheng, Xicheng, Haidian, Chaoyang, Fengtai, Changping, Daxing, Huairou, Pinggu, etc.

历史 history

北京已经有三千多年历史，最早可以追溯到公元前的秦汉时期，曾有辽、金、元、明、清五个朝代和中华民国（北洋政府时期）在此定都，北京与西安、洛阳、南京并称为中国的"四大古都"。

Beijing has been an inhabited city for more than three thousand years, dating back to the Qin and Han Dynasties. Historically, Beijing was a capital city in the Liao, Jin, Yuan, Ming and Qing Dynasties, and the Republic of China administrated by the Beiyang government. Together with Xi'an, Luoyang, Nanjing, Beijing is one of the four ancient cities in China.

教育 education

北京是中国的教育重镇，是全国教育最发达的地区之一，特别是高等教育，拥有全国数量最多的重点大学。坐落于北京的著名学府有：北京大学、清华大学、中国人民大学、北京航空航天大学、北京师范大学、中国传媒大学、北京电影学院、中央戏剧学院等。

Beijing is arguably the heart of the Chinese education system, especially higher education. It is home to many prestigious academic institutions, including Peking University, Tsinghua University, Renmin University of China, Beihang University, Beijing Normal University, Communication University of China, Beijing Film Academy, and The Central Academy of Drama, etc.

北京烤鸭 Beijing roast duck

北京饮食文化历史悠久，种类繁多。北京烤鸭、豆汁、涮肉、炸酱面、爆肚、驴打滚、豌豆黄等都是北京美食的代表，其中，北京烤鸭最为家喻户晓，在中国各地都大受欢迎。北京烤鸭原是宫廷食品，采用优质的北京鸭，用果木烤制而成，色泽金黄，外酥里嫩。辅以葱丝、黄瓜、甜面酱，与薄饼和削片的鸭肉、鸭皮一起食用，肉香四溢，肥而不腻。

As a well-known ancient city of history and culture, Beijing traditional food also has a long historical standing, embracing diverse tastes. Beijing roast duck, fermented soya-bean milk, Beijing hot pot, noodles with soybean paste, quick-fried tripe, rolling donkey and pea flour cake are representatives. Among them, Beijing roast duck is the most well-known tasty food and loved by the masses nationwide. Initially, Beijing roast duck was a royal dish. It was made of high-quality Beijing duck and roasted with fruit trees. It is golden in color, crisp outside and tender inside. Accompanied by shredded onions, cucumbers and sweet flour paste, it is eaten with pancakes, sliced duck meat and duck skin. The meat is fragrant, fat but not greasy.

旅游 Tourism

作为中国的首都，以及拥有悠久历史的古都，北京有着丰富的文化旅游资源，在世界文明史上有着重要的地位和国际影响力。北京著名的旅游景点有很多，例如天安门、人民英雄纪念碑、奥运场馆鸟巢和水立方、圆明园等。其中，北京拥有六项世界遗产，被列入《世界遗产名录》，是世界上拥有文化遗产最多的城市。

Beijing, the capital of China, is a time-honored ancient city and has rich cultural tourism resources. The city plays an important role and boasts a strong international influence on global civilization. Yet it's known as much for its abundant tourism resources, such as the Tian'anmen Square, Monument to the People's Heroes, Olympic venues like the Bird's Nest stadium, Water Cube, and Old Summer Palace. Six world heritage sites in Beijing are inscribed in the "World Heritage List". Undoubtedly, Beijing is the city with the most cultural heritages in the world.

四、课后思考 After class thinking

1. 你去过北京吗？北京令你印象最深刻的是什么？

Have you ever been to Beijing？ What impressed you most？

2. 你所在的国家的首都是哪里？有什么样的文化特色？

Where is the capital city in your country？ What are the cultural characteristics？

五、互动时间 Interaction time

1. 以下是电影《甲方乙方》中的经典片段，大家可以观摩影片，然后试着表演出来。

The following two classic parts are picked from *The Dream Factory*. Watch it and perform the content in the form of role play.

片段 1：

姚远：你看，那位先生，一看就是一大款，有钱，而且还是正道来的，称得上是仪表堂堂，财大气粗吧！

周北雁：就是，你看那西服穿在他身上多合适啊，就跟长在他身上似的。

姚远：再看先生那手，一看就是没干过活的，多细多长啊，准是弹钢琴的。

周北雁：嗯，真像。

姚远：再看人家怎么掏钱包，你看你看，单用二指这么轻轻一夹，神不知鬼不觉……

周北雁：哎哎，那位先生好像掏的不是自己的钱包。

姚远：喂，小偷……抓小偷。

Part 1：

Yao Yuan： Look at that Sir, he is definitely wealthy. And he must earn money in the right way. What a dignified rich man！

Zhou Beiyan： Yeah, the suit must have been perfectly customized for him.

Yao Yuan： Look at his long slender fingers, he must live in clover. Maybe he is a pianist.

Zhou Beiyan：Yes.

Yao Yuan：Look at how he picks a wallet，just taking it easily with two fingers．No one notices.

Zhou Beiyan：Ah！The sir takes others' wallet not his！

Yao Yuan：Hey！Thief！Grab him！

片段2：

周北雁：我美吗？

厨师：美美美。

周北雁：那你喜欢我吗？

厨师：喜欢，喜欢，你别馋我了。

梁子：你到底跟那个胖子说了句什么话呀？

姚远：你们问不出来。

周北雁：胖哥哥，能把你知道的秘密都告诉我吗？

厨师：能。

周北雁：那姚先生跟你说什么了？说吧。

厨师：嘿嘿嘿，打死我也不说。

周北雁：行，敬酒不吃吃罚酒，那你就等着上刑吧，胖子。

厨师：哎，不是。

Part 2：

Zhou Beiyan：Am I charming?

Chef：Yes！You are so beautiful！

Zhou Beiyan：Do you crush on me?

Chef：Yeah！

Liang Zi：What did you talk to the fat chef?

Yao Yuan：I won't tell you.

Zhou Beiyan：Cutie，could you tell me your secret?

Chef：Absolutely.

Zhou Beiyan：What did Mr. Yao say to you?

Chef：Hey – hey – hey！I won't talk even if I am going to die.

Zhou Beiyan：OK. Carrot or stick，it's your pick！

Chef：No，no！I don't mean it.

2. 学习并演唱2008年北京奥运会倒计时100天推广歌曲《北京欢迎你》的片段。

Learn the song clip "Welcome to Beijing"，a feature song for the 100-day countdown of the 2008 Summer Olympics.

北京欢迎你

作词：林夕

作曲：小柯

我家大门常打开　开怀容纳天地
岁月绽放青春笑容　迎接这个日期
天大地大都是朋友　请不用客气
画意诗情带笑意　只为等待你
北京欢迎你　像音乐感动你
让我们都加油去超越自己
北京欢迎你　有梦想谁都了不起
有勇气就会有奇迹
北京欢迎你　为你开天辟地
流动中的魅力充满着朝气
北京欢迎你　在太阳下分享呼吸
在黄土地刷新成绩

Welcome to Beijing

Lyricist：Lin Xi

Composer：Xiao Ke

My doors are always open，we're open for the world
Time flies with youthful smiles，all waiting to greet this day
Under the sky，everyone'll be our guest，so just be at home

Nice scenery with smiling faces, all awaiting there for you

Welcome to Beijing, touching you like this melody

Let's excel and try our best

Welcome to Beijing, dreamers are forerunners

Miracles are for those daring to try

Welcome to Beijing, we built these all for you

Flow with charm, refreshed and energized

Welcome to Beijing, let's take a breath beneath the sun

Let's set our new records on this Soil

下 编

奇幻武侠

Volume III
Martial Arts Fantasy

　　中国电影中的奇幻世界大多由历史传说和神话故事构成。通过这些电影作品，一方面可以看到中国电影发展中的多元化题材和纵横捭阖的创作视野，另一方面也可以激发学生对中国历史和中国文化的兴趣，从而以电影为窗口，进入上下五千年的神秘东方世界。

The fantasy world depicted in Chinese films mostly originates from historical legends and mythologies. We hope that these films would inspire you to learn about diverse genres of Chinese films. We trust too that increased creativity over the past years will succeed in generating more interest in Chinese history and traditional culture, even persuading one to explore the country in the eastern world, China, with a history of nearly 5,000 years.

第八单元
哪吒之魔童降世

本单元重点

1.了解电影《哪吒之魔童降世》的艺术特色
2.了解《封神演义》的基本知识

本单元难点

1.分析本片中的人物形象
2.分析电影"逆天改命"的主题

Unit 8
Ne Zha

Key points

1. Learn about the artistic characteristics of *Ne Zha*
2. Learn about the basic information on *The Investiture of the Gods*

Difficult points

1. Analyze character images portrayed in this film
2. Analyze the theme of "changing doomed destiny" exalted in this film

《哪吒之魔童降世》：东方英雄逆天改命

Ne Zha：**Oriental Hero Changed Doomed Destiny**

一、丝路放映厅 Silk Road screen hall

导演：饺子（原名：杨宇）

编剧：饺子

配音：吕艳婷/囧森瑟夫/瀚墨/陈浩

类型：动画电影

制片国家/地区：中国大陆

上映日期：2019 - 07 - 26

片长：110 分钟

英文名：*Ne Zha*

Director：Jiao Zi（original name：Yang Yu）

Screenwriter：Jiao Zi

Voice cast：Lü Yanting/Joseph/Han Mo/Chen Hao

Type：Animation

Production country/region：Chinese mainland

Release date：July 26，2019

Length：110 minutes

English name：*Ne Zha*

主要获奖 Major awards

第 16 届中国动漫金龙奖：最佳动画长片金奖、最佳动画导演奖、最佳动画编剧奖、最佳动画配音奖

第 35 届大众电影百花奖：最佳编剧奖

第 33 届中国电影金鸡奖：最佳美术片

The 16th China Animation Golden Dragon Award：Best Animation Feature Film Gold Award, Best Animation Director Award, Best Animation Screenplay Award and Best Dubbed Anime Award

The 35th Hundred Flowers Award：Best Screenplay Award

The 33rd China Film Golden Rooster Award：Best Animated Feature

剧情梗概 Plot synopsis

上古时期，天地灵气孕育出一颗混元珠，能量无比。元始天尊将其炼化成灵珠和魔丸，交予太乙真人看管。魔丸所代表的邪恶力量坚不可摧，于是天尊对魔丸设下天劫咒：三年后，天雷降临，摧毁魔丸。灵珠本应投胎成为陈塘关总兵李靖的第三个儿子——哪吒，但申公豹从中作怪，使得进入哪吒体内的灵珠被调包成魔丸。而灵珠则在海底龙王和申公豹的阴谋下，被放入龙王儿子敖丙的体内，唯有此举，才能够让龙族脱离海底炼狱，进入仙界。哪吒因体内的魔丸屡屡闯祸，被世人当作妖怪来对待。机缘巧合下，同样孤独的敖丙和哪吒成为朋友。哪吒三岁生日宴上，敖丙的身份暴露，因为拯救家族的责任被迫作出冰封陈塘关的抉择。在哪吒的影响下，敖丙迷途知返。三年时间已到，天雷下凡，哪吒与敖丙联手共同抵抗命运，成为彼此的知己。

In ancient time, a chaos pearl, birthed from primordial essences, begins siphoning energies voraciously. Due to its ability to absorb energy, Yuanshi Tianzun separates the pearl into two opposite components：the spirit pearl and the demon orb, and dispatches his disciple Taiyi Zhenren to subdue the sentient pearl. Eventually, Tianzun placed a heavenly curse upon the demon orb for its invincible evil power：in three years' time it would be destroyed by a heaven thunder. The spirit pearl should have been reincarnated as Ne Zha, the third son of Li Jing, the general of Chentang Pass. But Shen Gongbao did something wrong, the spirit pearl that entered Ne Zha's body was changed into a demon orb. The spirit pearl was put into the body of Ao Bing, the son of the Dragon King, under the conspiracy of the Dragon King and Shen Gongbao. Only by doing so, could the dragon family escape from the abyssal purgatory and enter the fairyland. Ne Zha was treated as a monster by the world because of his evil pills.

By chance, Ao Bing and Ne Zha, who were also lonely, became friends. At Ne Zha's third birthday party, Ao Bing's identity was revealed, and he was forced to make the choice of freezing Chentang Pass because of his responsibility to save the family. Under the influence of Ne Zha, Ao Bing went astray. Three years later, when a heaven thunder came down to earth, Ne Zha and Ao Bing joined hands to fight against the destiny and became each other's confidants.

重点词汇 Important vocabularies

摧毁	cuīhuǐ	v.	destroy
阴谋	yīnmóu	n.	conspiracy
龙王	Lóngwáng	n.	the Dragon King
朋友	péng·you	n.	friend
生日	shēngrì	n.	birthday
责任	zérèn	n.	responsibility
命运	mìngyùn	n.	destiny

例句 Example sentences

1. 地震几乎摧毁了整个城市。

The earthquake almost destroyed the entire city.

2. 真相背后的阴谋让人心惊胆战。

The conspiracy behind the truth is frightening.

3. 龙王在中国是吉祥的象征。

The Dragon King is worshipped as a propitious guardian deity in China.

4. 他是我很要好的朋友。

He is my best friend.

5. 十月一日是中国的生日。

October 1st is the birthday of the People's Republic of China.

6. 勇于承担责任才是成年人的行为。

Adults should shoulder their own responsibility.

7. 你的命运由你自己书写。

Your destiny should be determined by yourself.

语言练习 Language practices

请为以下句子选择合适的词语进行填空。

Please fill in the blanks with the appropriate words for the following sentences.

1. 向（　　　　）祈求下雨，是中国民间的传统仪式。

It is a traditional sacrificial activity to pray to the（　　　　）to dispense rain.

2. 我们现在看到的计划，只是这个（　　　　）的一部分。

The plan we learn about now is just a part of the（　　　　）.

3. 能力越大，（　　　　）越大。

With great power comes great（　　　　）.

4. 哪吒把敖丙看作自己最亲密的（　　　　）。

Ne Zha considers Ao Bing his closest（　　　　）.

5. 这件事情的发生，改变了他一生的（　　　　）。

This incident changed the（　　　　）of his life.

6. 每年过（　　　　），我都能收到很多礼物。

On my（　　　　）every year, I get a lot of gifts.

7. 这次的失败，几乎（　　　　）了他的自信心。

His confidence is almost（　　　　）for the failure.

二、丝路大讲堂 Silk Road lecture hall

【导演特色】Featuring director

饺子，原名杨宇，1980 年出生于四川省泸州市。原本毕业于四川大学华西药学院的他，因为自己对动画的热爱，走上了动画创作之路。2008 年，饺子创作首部动画短片《打，打个大西瓜》，该片获得中国动漫金龙奖，在柏林国际短片电影节等国内外重要电影节上也获得奖项。2009 年，"饺克力"工作室成立。2019 年，历经五年时间精心筹备的动画长片《哪吒之魔童降世》上映，最终获得 50 亿元人民币的票房，位列中国影史票房第二。饺子导演的作品叙事通俗易懂，人物语言简单直白、活泼有趣。但是，其作品又具有深刻的主题含义，打破了观众对于动漫作品"低幼化""儿童化"的刻板印象。短片《打，打个大西瓜》仅仅 16 分钟，表现出强烈的反战精神。《哪吒之魔童降世》更是对家喻户晓的哪吒故事进行了符合当代性的全新演绎，强调了不向命运屈服的自主精神。饺子将大众化、娱乐性与其主题的丰富性融合在一起，这在中国动画电影历史上起到了承前启后的重要作用。

Jiao Zi, also known as Yang Yu, was born in Luzhou City in Sichuan Province. He graduated from West China School of Pharmacy, Sichuan University, but transferred to animation creation due to his fascination for the art. In 2008, Jiao Zi created the first animated short film *See Through*, which won the China Animation Golden Dragon Award, and also won awards at important film festivals at home and abroad, such as the Berlin International Short Film Festival. In 2009, "Jokelate" studio was established. In 2019, the animated feature film *Ne Zha*, which had been carefully prepared for five years, was released and finally won 5 billion yuan at the box office, ranking the second in Chinese film history. The story depicted in his films unfolds with easy to understand, plain but captivating lines. Moreover, his works are exceptional. His versatile imagery entertains the young while also tantalizing the minds of the mature. *See Through*, the 16-minute short anti-war cartoon, expresses an aversion to war. *Ne Zha* is the unique 21st century reinterpretation based on the well-known mythology of Ne Zha, conveying the independent spirt of rebelling against one's doomed destiny. Jiao Zi combines popularity and entertainment with the richness of its theme, which plays an important role in the history of Chinese animation film.

【想象力美学】The aesthetics of imagination

《哪吒之魔童降世》立足于中国古老神话的传统基础，充分发挥想象力，将原本只存在于书中与民间传说的仙界幻境、魔界炼狱等奇观异境，通过三维动画技术进行现代影像转化，营造出具有鲜明中国特色的视觉图景。一方面，片中 CG 长镜头的大量运用，摇镜头的缓慢变化，在古典悠然的意境中，将山水之间的陈塘关呈现于观众眼前，表现出如中国文化细水长流般的运动感与流动性；另一方面，"山河社稷图"作为本片独创的场景，以其独特的意境和灵动的特征俘获了观众。"以笔运景"的调度设计，表现出了山水画般的写意风格和游戏化的趣味。本片成功地借助现代动画技术，让观众在电影中一览中国古典仙境，感受视听奇观。

Adapted from the mythological figure *Ne Zha*, director Jiao Zi unleashes imagination to visualize the Heaven and Hell which only exists in literatures and folklores by the virtue of 3D animation, presenting audiences with a visual feast with Chinese characteristics. In terms of photographic techniques, inserts of CG long shots are employed with the slow-paced camera, which allows audiences to be immersed and to witness the incredible scenery of Chentang Pass inhabited within mountains and rivers. When it comes to film settings in particular, the imaginary utopia portrayed in the "Painting of Mountains and Rivers" grabs people's attention for its breathtaking spots and dynamic aesthetics. With the stroke of the "Landscape Brush", the film conveys the freehand brushwork in Chinese Landscape Paintings and adds a gaming appeal. Indispensably, *Ne Zha* allows audiences to witness a Chinese classical wonderland with the extraordinary visual and audio effects.

【哪吒】 Ne Zha

本片的主人公哪吒，是中国经典文学作品《封神演义》中的主要人物之一。中国民间一直有"哪吒闹海"的传奇故事。"哪吒"作为人物原型，在中国可以说是深入人心。1979 年，上海美术电影制片厂的二维动画《哪吒闹海》上映，大获成功，哪吒小英雄的形象被大众接受。

哪吒形象：保留了哪吒乾坤圈和混天绫的设计，但是《哪吒之魔童降世》中的哪吒在形象上有较大差别。传统的哪吒唇红齿白，眉目间充满英气，是正气挺拔的少年形象。而本片中的哪吒在外形上则多了一分痞气。黑眼圈、残缺的牙齿，走路时双手插袋一摇一摆，让这个哪吒成了镇上人见人厌、避之不及的"魔丸"。

故事重构：以现代化叙事对哪吒故事进行颠覆式的重构和改写。哪吒从疾恶如仇的小英雄形象转变为反英雄的身份设定。同样是以"对抗权威"为主题，传统故事里的哪吒和父亲李靖之间的仇恨、哪吒和龙王之子敖丙之间的善恶分明，在本片中都进行了更为复杂和立体的人物关系处理。本片不但将父亲李靖转变为一位疼爱孩子、引领哪吒勇敢改变自己命运的人生导师，更是让敖丙作为灵珠转世和魔丸哪吒之间展开了一段感人的友谊。叙事重点放在哪吒虽然"生而为魔"但"不屈服于命运"的成长上，从个人对父权的反抗上升至个人对命运的反抗。

The protagonist Ne Zha depicted in this film is adapted from one of the major characters of *The Investiture of the Gods*, a classical Chinese literature work. The legend of "Ne Zha Conquers the Dragon King" is well known by the Chinese nation. In 1979, *Ne Zha Conquers the Dragon King*, a Chinese animated fantasy film produced by Shanghai Animation Film Studio, was released and achieved great success. Therefore, Chinese audiences are familiar with the little superhero.

The appearance of Ne Zha: The film keeps the initial image of Ne Zha who equips the

Qiankun hoop and red armillary sash, with an emphasis on Ne Zha's new screen image. The traditional Ne Zha has red lips and white teeth, and his eyebrows and eyes are full of heroism. He is a upright young man. However, Ne Zha in this film has a ruffian temperament in appearance. With dark circles under his eyes and broken teeth, he put his hands in his pockets and shook them when walking. He became a demon orb that people in the town hated and avoided.

Story reconstruction: In this film, the modernization narrative device is employed to depict a disruptive image of Ne Zha, from the little superhero who hates evil to the atypical hero. Derived from the theme of "resistance", unlike Ne Zha fundamentally opposing the relationship between father and son, resenting the Dragon King and being kind to Ao Bing (the son of the Dragon King), the film reinterprets the initial plot setting to present more enriching and persuading roles. Thereby, Li Jing is transformed to be a doting father and life mentor, advising Ne Zha "You are the only one who controls what you become". On top of this, the touching friendship between Ne Zha (the demon orb) and Ao Bing (the spirit pearl) is developed. The main storyline unfolds based on the resistance to doomed fate that Ne Zha was born to be a "demon". Unlike the traditional plot setting, which focuses on the bad relationship between father and son, the twist in the plot is Ne Zha rebelling against his destiny.

【与哪吒形象有关的影视作品】Films and televisions related to the image of Ne Zha

(1)《哪吒闹海》(1979 年):我国第一部彩色宽银幕动画长片,由上海美术电影制片厂制作出品。本片是中华人民共和国成立三十周年献礼影片,获得了第三届大众电影百花奖最佳动画电影奖、第二届菲律宾马尼拉国际电影节特别奖等奖项,是中国动画学派的代表作。

(2)《西游记》(1986 年):中央电视台版本的电视剧《西游记》是最经典的《西游记》影视化版本,主角是唐僧、孙悟空、猪八戒、沙僧师徒四人,哪吒以配角的身份出现。

(3)《封神榜》(1990 年):改编自明代长篇小说《封神演义》,哪吒在此剧中的形象由儿童变为少年。

(4)《封神榜》(2001 年):香港 TVB 电视台出品的 40 集电视剧,哪吒一角由香港影星陈浩民扮演，哪吒完全成为成年人的形象。

（5）《哪吒传奇》（2003 年）：作为长篇电视动画，二维动画《哪吒传奇》共 52 集，播出以后少年英雄小哪吒的形象受到了小朋友们的喜欢。

（6）《新神榜：哪吒重生》（2021 年）：哪吒在三千年后转世重生，来到现代社会发生了一段惊心动魄的故事，东方的古典神韵和现代"朋克"风格相结合。本片在 2021 年春节期间上映，带来了震撼的 3D 视听效果。

（1）*Ne Zha Conquers the Dragon King*（1979）：the representative work of Chinese animation school as well as the first colorful widescreen animated fantasy film produced by Shanghai Animation Film Studio, was released to celebrate the 30th anniversary of the founding of the People's Republic of China. It has received a variety of awards, including the 3rd Hundred Flowers Festival Award and the Special Award at the 2nd Manila International Film Festival in 1983. It is the reprresentative work of the Chinese Animation School.

（2）*Journey to the West*（1986）：The CCTV version of *Journey to the West* is the most classic film and television version, Main casts include Tang Sanzang, Sun Wukong, Zhu Bajie, Sha Seng, with other casts, like Ne Zha.

（3）*The Legend of Deification*（1990）：adapted from the long fiction *The Investiture of the Gods* of the Ming Dynasty. Ne Zha is portrayed as a teenager not a child.

（4）*Gods of Honour*（2001）：a television series with 40 episodes, was first aired on TVB Jade in Hong Kong. Ne Zha is depicted as an adult played by Benny Chan, a Hong Kong male star.

（5）*The Legend of Ne Zha*（2003）：a 2D animated cartoon series with 52 episodes. Since its release, Ne Zha, the little superhero, has been touted by children nationwide.

（6）*New Gods*：*Ne Zha Reborn*（2021）：Ne Zha was reincarnated and reborn three thousand years later and came to the modern society. And then a thrilling story happened. The classical charm of the East was combined with the modern punkstyle. This film was released during the 2021 Spring Festival, bringing a shocking 3D audio-visual effect.

【"三幕式"结构】Three-act structure

在当代商业化、市场化的背景之下，本片借鉴已经成熟的好莱坞商业电影的剧作模式，使得影片叙事节奏流畅，可看性更强。本片的叙事呈现出经典的"三幕式"剧作结构。

第一幕：明确剧中主要人物，并介绍故事发生背景。先以太乙旁白来介绍故事发生背景，埋下三年后天雷下凡这一伏笔。利用魔丸和灵珠构建出哪吒和敖丙之间的人物关系。

第二幕：遭遇危机及抗争过程。哪吒因为魔丸身份被世人唾弃，虽想要改变，但总是无功而返。从捉拿夜叉、解救女孩到遭百姓误会，导演通过递进式叙事，使哪吒和百姓间的误会越来越深，直到申公豹将魔丸真相告知哪吒，哪吒达到愤怒的顶峰而大开杀戒，推动影片核心矛盾的爆发。

第三幕：解决危机。一切误会被解除，哪吒救下陈塘关和所有百姓，准备独自一人面对天劫。而此时，敖丙受到哪吒的感化，放下家族执念，与哪吒共同反抗命运。在影片的最后，导演饺子运用"最后一分钟营救"的剧作手法，让太乙用七色莲保住两人的魂魄，免于一死。而百姓向哪吒跪拜，表示哪吒最终凭借自己的努力，改变了世人心中的成见，再次点明影片的主题。

影片取材自中国传统故事，融合了好莱坞经典戏剧性叙事结构，并以"我命由我不由天"为影片的主流价值观，使得影片在传承中华优秀传统文化的同时更具有大众性和国际性。

Affected by the market appeal of commercial films produced by the Hollywood studio, *Ne Zha* adopts its developed classical screenplay structure (three-act play approach), unfolding plots appropriately to produce a smooth flow of action.

Act one: it establishes the dramatic premise to introduce protagonists and background information. Taiyi, the storyteller, reveals the destiny of Ne Zha who will be destroyed by a heaven thunder three years later. The relationship between the demon orb and the spirit pearl also hints at the intertwined destinies between Ne Zha and Ao Bing.

Act two: confrontation consists of misunderstanding and rebellion. Ne Zha is resented by villagers for his demonic nature, yet despite his determination to change, he always failed. As the plot develops, Ne Zha drives off the Sea Yaksha and saves the little girl, but his action is misunderstood by local villagers, while the escalating conflict builds to its maximum tension in the climax when the truth that Ne Zha is the demon orb reborn is revealed by Shen Gongbao. Ne Zha turns demonic, promoting the outbreak of the film's core contradiction.

Act three: resolution. All misunderstandings are resolved. Ne Zha rescues Chentang

Pass and all the villagers, and prepares to face the heavenly tribulation alone. At this time, Ao Bing is influenced by Ne Zha, lets go of his family obsession, and joins hands to fight against destiny with Ne Zha. Director Jiao Zi follows "the last-minute rescue" narratives, allowing Taiyi to keep the souls of Ne Zha and Ao Bing intact by using the Prismatic Lotus. The story ends with the townsfolk kneeling before Ne Zha, which means Ne Zha finally changes the prejudice in people's minds with his own efforts. The theme of the film is highlighted again.

The film adapted from traditional Chinese folk legends, uses the Hollywood classical dramatic narrative formula, and exalts the "I am the master of my destiny" mainstream values, thereby popularizing traditional Chinese culture while adding an international appeal.

【知命改命】 Know your destiny and change your destiny

古典文本的哪吒故事中，"削肉还母，剔骨还父"始终是核心情节，也是哪吒反叛精神内核的体现，这是一个古希腊式的悲剧故事。而电影《哪吒之魔童降世》在主题上表达的是一个极具现代精神的人文主题——"我命由我不由天"，注重个体的自我关注与自我价值的实现。影片中的哪吒不再是原作《封神演义》中"灵珠子"转世的神孩，而是魔丸转世的魔王。因此，哪吒自出生起就被世人当作怪物，被世人误会、谩骂。面对世人内心的成见、命中注定的天雷劫，哪吒虽然有过自我怀疑，但没有自甘堕落成为魔王，反而掌握了自己的命运，拯救了陈塘关的百姓们，更是以自己对抗命运的决心唤起了敖丙心中的善念。"改命"只是表层，"知命改命"才是影片传达出的核心意义。我是谁，不是由别人定义的；我是谁，只能由自己定义。

Classic records unfold the sort of "Greek tragedy" that Ne Zha sacrificed himself by committing suicide and "returning his flesh and bones to his parents". Its theme reflects the meaning of "resistance". While the "resistance" in *Ne Zha*, a more current human theme, is the struggle of a special individual against a prescribed fate — "I am the master of my destiny", with the attention of building and achieving an individual's self-recognition and self-esteem. Unlike the divine boy, a reincarnation of the spirit pearl, portrayed in the literary source *The Investiture of the Gods*, Ne Zha in the film is a reincarnation of the demon orb. Thus, Ne Zha has been nevertheless misunderstood, resented and treated as a demon child by the townsfolk since his birth. The prejudice and awaited doomed heaven thunder strikes press him to doubt himself, but not overwhelm him, instead he finally chooses to become himself and control his own destiny, save the villagers of Chentang Pass, even awaken Ao Bing to be good with his determination to break the shackles of destiny. "Change your destiny" is adulated in the film, while "know your destiny and change your destiny" is the core value the film wishes to convey. I am the master of my destiny! Not anyone else.

【山河社稷图】 The painting of Mountains and Rivers

出自中国古典小说《封神演义》，本是女娲的法宝，后授予二郎神杨戬用于收服恶怪袁洪。本片中，山河社稷图提供了一个惊人的视觉奇观，太乙真人用"笔"（法术）运景，随意改变空间里的构成元素，实则展现的是意念和想象的力量。这是一种游戏化的空间设定，太乙真人利用山河社稷图中的空间，骗哪吒入图练习武艺和法术，实际上是囚禁了哪吒。但山河社稷图不是冷冰冰的监狱，图中的世界犹如现实中的游乐园，从云霄直下的刺激过山车到清澈河流上的荷花漂流，以及哪吒、敖丙、太乙真人、申公豹四人的混战，都做成了漫画版的"弹球大战"游戏。山河社稷图内游戏化的场景设定，使得电影逢合网络时代成长起来的年青一代的审美需求。

The painting of Mountains and Rivers is from the Chinese classical novel *The Investiture of the Gods*. It is originally owned by Nüwa, and later she gave it to the god of Erlang Yang Jian to capture the demon Yuan Hong. In the film, the painting provides a breathtaking visual feast. The immortal Taiyi Zhenren establishes scenes inside the fantasy world of the painting, which can be changed freely, with the use of the magic landscape brush. Similar to a gamelike space setting, it conveys the great power of one's will and imagination. Taiyi Zhenren utilizes the amazing space setting to persuade Ne Zha to train immortal techniques, but meant to imprison him to avoid bringing chaos to the village. Yet, the painting does not serve as a depressing prison at all. The remarkable world inside performs like an amusement park with the CG techniques, presenting a thrilling roller coaster from the upper air down to the ground, a cozy raft sitting on a lotus on a crystal river, and an animated "pinball" game between four characters, namely, Ne Zha, Ao Bing, Taiyi Zhenren, and Shen Gongbao. Thus, the gaming space setting embedded in the painting fulfills the tastes of the growing younger generation amid the rapid development of the internet.

互动讨论 Interactive discussion

1. 结合剧情和老师的讲解，试着讲讲你对这几句话的理解。

Combining the plot with the teacher's explanation, try to talk about your understandings of the following sentences.

（1）人心中的成见就像一座大山，任你如何努力都无法搬动它。

Humans have enough prejudice to build a mountain, one that remains immovable no matter how hard you try.

（2）我命由我不由天；是魔是仙，我自己说了才算！

I am the master of my destiny! I'm the one who decides whether I'm an immortal or a demon!

2. 回答以下问题，并进行讨论。

Answer the following questions and have a discussion.

（1）影片中，敖丙为什么要冰封陈塘关？

In the film, why does Ao Bing try to bury all Chentang Pass?

（2）你最喜欢影片中哪一个人物？结合影片谈谈你对哪吒这一人物形象的理解。

Which one is your favorite character in the film? In your opinion, describe your view of Ne Zha.

三、延伸阅读 Extended reading

1. 哪吒文化 Cultures related to Ne Zha

《封神演义》 *The Investiture of the Gods*

人们所熟知的哪吒的人物形象和故事主体，主要来源于明代的长篇小说《封神演义》。此书相传由明代作家许仲琳所创作，全书共一百回，以周武王姬发伐纣为主要内容。商纣王在狐妖附体的苏妲己的诱惑下，沉溺酒色，执政暴虐。周武王姬发在姜子牙的辅佐下完成讨伐纣王的大业，夺取天下，在封神台封神。

The well-known image and legend of Ne Zha is adapted from the literary source *The Investiture of the Gods*, a novel of the Ming Dynasty. It is said that the literature was written by Xu Zhonglin, with 100 chapters. The novel is a romanticized retelling of the overthrow of

King Zhou，the last ruler of the Shang Dynasty，by Ji Fa，who would establish the Zhou Dynasty in its place．Bewitched by his concubine Su Daji，who is actually a vixen spirit disguised as a beautiful woman，King Zhou of Shang oppresses his people and persecutes those who oppose him，including those who dare to speak up to him．Ji Fa（King Wu of Zhou），assisted by his strategist Jiang Ziya，rallies an army to overthrow the tyrant and restore peace and order．

哪吒祖庙 Ne Zha temple

道教神谱《三教源流搜神大全》中记载的哪吒是神兵神将的统帅，被玉帝封为"天帅元领袖"，是道教供奉的神仙之一。因此，国内及东南亚各地都有信仰哪吒的文化传统及祭拜仪式，还建有哪吒祖庙，供人祭拜，如台湾哪吒神庙、河南哪吒祖庙、四川哪吒庙、泰国哪吒庙等。

A Taoist book，*Comprehensive Collection of the Search for Divinities of the Three Doctrines*，records that Ne Zha is entitled to rule divine soldiers as the army leader "Marshal of the Central Altar"，canonized by the Jade Emperor，and that Ne Zha is also one of the Taoist gods．Hence，there are cultural traditions and sacrificial activities to worship Ne Zha in China and across Southeast Asia．Ne Zha temples for the devout are also built at home and abroad，such as Taiwan Ne Zha Temple，Henan Ne Zha Temple，Sichuan Ne Zha Temple，Thailand Ne Zha Temple，etc．

乾坤圈与混天绫 The Qiankun hoop and red armillary sash

乾坤圈与混天绫是哪吒的两大本命法宝，由哪吒的师傅太乙真人赠送。乾坤圈坚硬无比，摧毁力极强，可自由变换大小，具有翻江闹海的神力。传统哪吒故事中，乾坤圈是打死了龙王三太子敖丙的武器，也是伐纣大战中所向披靡的利器。在《哪吒之魔童降世》中，乾坤圈是太乙真人用来锁住魔丸邪性的工具。混天绫与乾坤圈一对，可自动绑人且随意变换大小，小说《封神演义》中提到哪吒洗澡时混天绫引得地动山摇，威力巨大，整个海底龙宫都在晃动。

The Qiankun hoop and red armillary sash are two powerful weapons given by the Master Taiyi Zhenren to his disciple Ne Zha．The Qiankun hoop in a flexible shape is extremely impregnable to destroy everything，and can be used to bring chaos to the sea．The traditional legends tell that Ne Zha uses the Qiankun hoop to kill Ao Bing, the third son of the Dragon King, and to help Ji Fa (King Wu of Zhou) defeat King Zhou as well. In *Ne Zha*, the Qiankun hoop is adopted by Taiyi Zhenren to suppress Ne Zha's demonic nature. With the accompaniment of the red armillary sash, the Qiankun hoop largely unleashes its power with adjustable shapes to tie someone freely. *The Investiture of the Gods* documents that Ne Zha once used it to shower which caused so much havoc that it almost caused the Dragon Palace to collapse.

风火轮与火尖枪 The wind-and-fire wheels and fire-tipped spear

在《封神演义》等文学作品中，哪吒的风火轮系太乙真人所授，既是飞行工具，又是战斗兵器。风火轮踩于足下，便能够轮上起火、足下生风，腾云驾雾、日行千里。在电影《哪吒之魔童降世》中，太乙真人的坐骑在送给哪吒后变成了风火轮（该坐骑可根据意念变成各种形态）。火尖枪与风火轮相配，主攻近战，哪吒在山河社稷图修炼期间从师父太乙真人处获得此物。

Some literary works, like *The Investiture of the Gods*, mention that Taiyi Zhenren gave the wind-and-fire wheels (a fire-wheel and a wind-wheel) to Ne Zha, which serves not only as a flying mount, but also as a combat weapon. In *Ne Zha*, the mount of Taiyi Zhenren is transformed to be wind-and-fire wheels when Taiyi gives it to Ne Zha due to it can be transformed according to its owner's characteristics. The wind-and-fire wheels and fire-tipped spear function as melee weapons, and the latter one is taken by Ne Zha from his master Taiyi Zhenren during he accepts initial training in the painting of Mountains and Rivers.

2. 商周时期 The era of the Shang and the Zhou Dynasties

青铜器 Bronze ware

商周时期，青铜器的冶炼和制造十分成熟，各种器具、礼器十分精美。影片中的结界兽便是取材于三星堆文化中的金面罩青铜人头像、青铜鹰形铃和青铜兽面具。而在哪吒三岁生辰宴这一场景中，陈塘关百姓们桌上所用的杯子便是商代常见的饮酒器——觚。

The era of the Shang and the Zhou Dynasties is generally known as the Bronze Age of China for the mature technology of bronze smelting and manufacturing. Numerous vessels, including ritual vessels, were quite exquisite. The two boundary beasts portrayed in *Ne Zha* are based on bronzes, namely the bronze human head wearing a golden mask, a bronze bird and a bronze animal mask, which were unearthed at the Sanxingdui culture, an archaeological site. Moreover, at Ne Zha's third birthday celebration, the cups on the tables for the people of Chentang Pass to drink from, are popular drinking vessels (gu) made in the Shang Dynasty.

甲骨文 Oracle-bone inscriptions

甲骨文是我们目前所知最早的成熟汉字，主要指商朝晚期王室用于占卜记事而在龟甲或兽骨上镌刻、写出的文字，具有对称、稳定的格局。虽然甲骨文的文字系统较为严密，但其作为原始图画文字，象形意义仍较为明显。2017 年 11 月 24 日，甲骨文成功入选《世界记忆名录》。

Oracle-bone inscriptions (OBI) are the earliest known form of Chinese characters engraved on oracle bones—animal bones or turtle plastrons. They were records of divinations and prayers to gods by late Shang royal people in a symmetrical and stable pattern. Despite OBI having already evolved into a mature character system, its pictorial nature accurately represents meaning. On November 24, 2017, OBI was successfully selected into the Memory of the World Register.

牧野之战 The battle of Muye

牧野之战是周武王伐纣的决胜战。因其发生在牧野（今河南淇县南、卫河以北，新乡市附近）而得名。牧野之战是中国历史上以少胜多、以弱胜强、先发制人的著名战例。这场战争象征着六百多年的商王朝被推翻，确立了西周王朝的统治。

The battle of Muye is the final battle between the rebel Zhou state and the reigning Shang Dynasty. It was named as "the battle of Muye" after the battleground Muye (now nearby Xinxiang City, South of Qixian County and north of Weihe Ricer in Henan Province). The battle of Muye is a famous example in Chinese history of defeating the many with the few, defeating the strong with the weak, and taking the initiative. The battle resulted in the fall of the Shang Dynasty that had ruled for over 600 years, and the beginning of the Xizhou Dynasty.

绘画 Silk paintings

周朝文献对于壁画的记载是比较丰富的，从史书上的各种记载，我们可以窥见当时壁画规模的巨大，但由于时代久远，均未流传至今。而流传下来的几幅战国帛画，特别是《人物龙凤图》《人物御龙图》，则代表了当时绘画的最高水平，从中我们也可以看出，中国画以线造型的特点已露端倪。

Abundant documents in the Zhou Dynasty attest to the widespread development of murals. However, due to their great age, they all have not all been preserved. Some silk paintings of the Warring States Period passed down to today, in particular, the "Silk Painting of a Lady, Dragon and Phoenix" and the "Silk Painting Depicting a Man Riding a Dragon", represent the marvelous painting technique at that time, and reflect the concept of line modeling in Chinese painting.

道教 Taoism

影片的背景设定是通过道教的神话世界观构建的，哪吒也是道家的守护神。混元珠也是符合道教中太极八卦的文化传统进行设定的。而影片中，元始天尊在魔丸上所施的天劫咒，是八卦中的震卦。而元始天尊正是道教"三清尊神"之一，在"三清尊神"中地位最高。

The plot setting is based on the framework of a Taoist mythological world, and the character Ne Zha is depicted based on a protective deity in Taoism as well. Aside from the chaos pearl, it fits the traditional culture in terms of Taiqi and Bagua, a heavenly curse on the demon orb cast by Yuanshi Tianzhun, who is the supreme one among the Three Pure Ones in Taoism, and is one of parts in Bagua called Zhen.

四、课后思考 After class thinking

1. 有许多电影都立足于中国传统文化，说说你在《哪吒之魔童降世》中都感受到了哪些中国传统文化元素。

Many films are based on Chinese traditional cultural. Talk about what elements of traditional Chinese culture you have felt in *Ne Zha*.

2. 说说你所在国家的经典神话故事。

Describe the classical mythologies in your country.

五、互动时间 Interaction time

看了各个版本的哪吒，相信你已经对哪吒形象印象深刻，下面就按照简笔画试着画出可爱的哪吒吧。

After being familiar with different images of Ne Zha，try to draw a stick figure of Ne Zha.

第九单元
功　夫

本单元重点

1.了解周星驰的艺术成就
2.了解中国香港的概况

本单元难点

1.了解"草根文化"及其特色
2.分析电影《功夫》中主人公阿星的英雄形象

Unit 9
Kung Fu Hustle

📢 Key points

1.Learn about the Stephen Chow's artistic success
2.Learn about the basic information on Hong Kong, China

📢 Difficult points

1.Learn about "grassroot culture" and its features
2.Analyze the protagonist Sing depicted as a hero in *Kung Fu Hustle*

《功夫》：高手又见高手

Kung Fu Hustle：**Master Battle**

一、丝路放映厅 Silk Road screen hall

导演：周星驰

编剧：周星驰/曾谨昌/霍昕/陈文强

主演：周星驰/黄圣依/陈国坤/元华

类型：剧情/武侠

制片国家/地区：中国内地

上映日期：2004 – 12 – 23 （中国大陆）/2015 – 01 – 15 （中国大陆3D）

片长：95 分钟

英文名：*Kung Fu Hustle*

Director：Stephen Chow

Screenwriter：Stephen Chow/Tsang Kan-cheung/Huo Xin/Chan Man-keung

Starring：Stephen Chow/Huang Shengyi/Danny Chan Kwok Kwan/Yuen Wah

Type：Drama/Martial Arts

Production country/region：Chinese mainland

Release date：December 23，2004 （Chinese mainland）/January 15，2015 （3D version Chinese mainland）

Length：95 minutes

English name：*Kung Fu Hustle*

主要获奖 Major awards

第24届香港电影金像奖：最佳电影、最佳男配角、最佳动作设计

第 42 届台湾电影金马奖：最佳剧情片、最佳导演、最佳女配角

The 24th Hong Kong Film Award：Best Film，Best Supporting Actor，Best Action Choreography

The 42nd Golden Horse Award：Best Feature Film，Best Director，Best Supporting Actress

剧情梗概 Plot synopsis

20 世纪 40 年代的中国，黑暗势力斧头帮独霸一方，成为远近闻名的黑帮。从小受欺负的小混混阿星（周星驰饰）想加入声势浩大的斧头帮，借此扬眉吐气。某天，阿星正在冒充斧头帮的成员在贫民窟猪笼城寨里敲诈，不料真正的斧头帮出现了。猪笼城寨的居民看似普通，实际上隐藏着不少武林高手。斧头帮想要将猪笼城寨变成自己的势力范围，遭到了居民们的奋力抵抗，失败而归。斧头帮带着一帮武林高手前来复仇，城寨中的居民们难以抵抗，节节败退。被激发出正义感的阿星想要帮助居民们，却势单力薄，力不从心，被"火云邪神"（梁小龙饰）打成重伤。在治疗过程中，阿星回忆起童年热心善良、乐于助人的自己，也记起了自己所练的武功"如来神掌"。城寨的居民发现，阿星有着极高的武功天赋以及惊人的恢复能力。最终，阿星也变成了武林高手，用"如来神掌"打败了江湖排名第一的"火云邪神"，帮助居民们战胜了邪恶的斧头帮。成为武林高手的阿星找回了从前的自己，也收获了与哑女纯真的爱情。

Set in China in the 1940s，various sinister gangs vie for power，the most feared one is the Axe Gang. A "wannabe" gangster Sing（played by Stephen Chow）aspires to join the notorious Axe Gang，as he has been bullied since he was little. One day，Sing comes to the Pigsty Alley impersonating members of the Axe Gang in order to extort money. Unexpectedly，the real Axe Gang appeared. The residents of the Pigsty Alley seem ordinary，but actually there are many martial arts masters hidden. The Axe Gang tried to turn the Pigsty Alley stronghold into their sphere of influence，but they are resisted by the residents and returned in failure. The Axe Gang come to revenge with a group of martial arts masters. The residents in the stronghold are unable to resist and retreated. Sing，who is inspired with a sense of justice，wants to help the residents，but he is weak and unable to do what he wanted. He is severely injured by the "Fire Cloud Evil God"（played by Liang Xiaolong）. In the process of treatment, Sing recalled his warm, kind and helpful childhood, and also remembered his martial arts "Buddha's Palm". The residents of the stronghold found that Sing has a very high martial arts talent and amazing recovery ability. In the end, Sing becomes a martial arts master, and defeats the No. 1 "Fire Cloud Evil God" in the Jianghu with the "Buddha's Palm", helping the residents defeat the evil Axe Gang. Sing, who becomes a martial arts master, finds his former self and gains pure love with the mute girl.

重点词汇 Important vocabularies

黑帮	hēibāng	*n.*	sinister gang
普通	pǔtōng	*adj.*	ordinary
隐藏	yǐncáng	*v.*	hide
武林	wǔlín	*n.*	Martial arts
高手	gāoshǒu	*n.*	master
打败	dǎbài	*v.*	defeat

例句 Example sentences

1. 近日，某市的黑帮团伙被警察剿灭。

Recently, a sinister gang which gathered in a city was wiped out by the police.

2. 普通人也有权利过幸福的一生。

There is no exception to the rule that people have a right to live happily, including the ordinary people.

3. 表面之下往往隐藏着真相。

The truth is always hidden.

4. 武林中流传着他的传说。

His legend is well-known in the Martial arts.

5. 高手之间的对决分外精彩。

The battle between masters is impressive.

6. 在决赛中打败对手，才能成为冠军。

People who defeat their rivals in the final of a competition emerge as winners.

语言练习 Language practices

请为以下句子选择合适的词语进行填空。

Please fill in the blanks with the appropriate words for the following sentences.

1. （　　　　　）之间总是惺惺相惜。

（　　　　　）always appreciate each other.

2. 他（　　　　　）着不可告人的秘密。

He's（　　　　　）an unspeakable secret.

3. 扫黑行动就是要坚决打击（　　　　　）。

Crime crackdown is meant to strictly address（　　　　　）.

4. 不要轻易被困难（　　　　　）。

Don't be（　　　　　）by difficulties.

5. 这款首饰的设计太过（　　　　　）了。

The design of the jewelry is quite（　　　　　）.

6. 凭着高超的武功，他在（　　　　　）中早已没有对手。

With（his）superb Kung fu, he is invincible in（　　　　　）.

二、丝路大讲堂 Silk Road lecture hall

【导演特色】 Featuring director

周星驰，1962 年出生于中国香港，著名男演员、导演、编剧、制作人。周星驰的"无厘头"喜剧风格对华语电影喜剧片的发展产生了深厚的影响，因此，他被影迷称为"星爷"。从影之初，周星驰出演了几部动作片。直到 1990 年，他在喜剧片《一本漫画闯天涯》中担任主演，确立了独特的"无厘头"表演风格。之后，周星驰主演的《赌圣》（1990 年）、《逃学威龙》（1991 年）、《整蛊专家》（1991 年）、《唐伯虎点秋香》（1993 年）等喜剧片大受欢迎，优秀的票房成绩使周星驰成为最"卖座"演员之一，与成龙、周润发并称为"双周一成"。从 1994 年的《国产凌凌漆》起，周星驰开始初执导筒，开始尝试自导自演，更加鲜明地确立了周氏喜剧风格。

其自导自演的代表作品有《大内密探零零发》（1996 年）、《食神》（1996 年）、《喜剧之王》（1999 年）、《少林足球》（2001 年）、《功夫》（2004 年）、《长江七号》（2005 年）等。近些年，周星驰退居幕后，主要担任制片人、编剧与导演，不再活跃于大银幕上，代表作品有《西游·降魔篇》（2013 年）、《美人鱼》（2015 年）、《新喜剧之王》（2019 年）等。在周星驰三十余年的喜剧之路中，他尝试了多样化的题材，包括对中国民间经典文学作品《西游记》改编的《大话西游》（1995 年）等系列作品。周星驰的电影虽然有着夸张的喜剧表达，但也具有强烈的写实主义和民族色彩。周星驰被喻为"东方卓别林"，和卓别林一样，周星驰的电影无论是古代题材还是都市题材，都将目光落到小人物在大环境下的成长和转变上，无论是落魄的古代小官、跑龙套的群众演员，还是被人类视为异类的美人鱼，周星驰都为电影中的主人公赋予了乐观、坚韧的生活态度。

Stephen Chow was born in Hong Kong China in 1962. He is a famous male actor, director, screenwriter, and film producer. His distinctive style of adding unique "Mo lei tau" (nonsensical) stories to comedy films generates a profound effect on Chinese comedy films. For that, his fans have nicknamed him "Xing Ye". In his early film career, he was involved in several action films as an extra. Since 1990, he acted in the title role in *My Hero*, and he formed his unique "Mo lei tau" performing style. Several comedy films followed in which he acted in the leading role, such as *All for the Winner* (1990), *Fight Back to School* (1991), *Tricky Brains* (1991), *Flirting Scholar* (1993) and these (roles) quickly earned him recognition. The remarkable box office takings suggest that he is the actor with a great box office appeal, and he is also touted to be on a par with Jackie Chan and Chow Yun-fat. In 1994, he made his debut film *From Beijing with Love*, marking the beginning of his director and actor interwoven career and optimizing his featured comedy style.

Representative of those he directed and starred in include *Forbidden City Cop* (1996), *The God of Cookery* (1996), *King of Comedy* (1999), *Shaolin Soccer* (2001), *Kung Fu Hustle* (2004) and *CJ 7* (2005), etc. Over the last years, Stephen Chow scarcely takes acting roles, preferring instead that of film producer, screenwriter, and director. His successes include *Journey to the West: Conquering the Demons* (2013), *The Mermaid* (2015), and *The New King of Comedy* (2019), etc. In his more than thirty-year career, he has produced various genres of films, including several adaptations, like *A Chinese Odyssey* (1995), adapted from the Chinese classical folk literature *Journey to the West*. Despite his method of over-exaggeration, his comedies depict the realistic Chinese nation in realism. Stephen Chow is touted the "Chinese Charlie Chaplin", due to his ancient or urban film resembling a Charlie Chaplin-style comedy, with the emphasis on the growth and transformation of the grassroots, portrayed as the depressed lord with minor authority, the extra actor, and the mermaid presented as an exotic creature in people's minds. However, director Chow depicts them to be optimistic and tenacious.

【"无厘头"喜剧】"Mo lei tau" comedy

"无厘头"一词，出自广东南海一带的方言，原意指"没有首尾的脊骨"。在俚语中，可以解释为无头绪、没有逻辑，说的话、做的事情使人难以理解，行为模式和说话没有明确的指向性，目的模糊。周星驰的电影擅长使用俚语，又设计了许多性格古怪、造型各异的人物，并且擅长对既定形象和经典故事进行改写，形成了一种陌生化的错位感，建立了"无厘头"的喜剧风格。在电影《功夫》中，有许多典型的"无厘头"风格的喜剧段落：

（1）凶狠的斧头帮：在最开始介绍斧头帮的时候，斧头帮独特的集体舞蹈和观众认知中警匪片、黑帮片严肃、凶狠的黑帮形象大相径庭，这是对观众认知经验的一种颠覆，也是对黑帮片的解构。在斧头帮帮主说自己"从来不杀女人"后，观众都以为鳄鱼帮帮主的女人能够逃过一劫，斧头帮帮主却出其不意地用枪将她击毙。跳舞与杀戮、"不杀女人"的口是心非形成了出其不意的喜剧效果。

（2）神秘的火云邪神：武林排名第一的火云邪神是被斧头帮重金请来的终极杀手。但是，火云邪神的出场并没有突出他的凶恶，一个戴着眼镜，穿着背心与短裤，脚上穿着拖鞋，坐在马桶上看报纸的秃顶老年人，和火云邪神武林高手的形象反差巨大。在阴森诡异的氛围下，火云邪神以这种日常化的形象出现，喜剧效果十足。此外，火云邪神的武功是蛤蟆功，影片使用逼真的电脑特效，当火云邪神匍匐在地上的时候，两腮鼓起，形似蛤蟆。中国功夫一般讲究写意，神似多于形似，这里将蛤蟆功以逼真的动物形态呈现出来，以夸张的肢体表现营造出独特的喜剧效果。

（3）阿星的单挑：阿星第一次来到猪笼城寨，敲诈没有成功，就想要找一个街坊单挑。先出来了一个小朋友，没想到打败了阿星。阿星就找了个看起来最矮的人，结果站起来是个巨人。后来，阿星只能找个大妈，没想到大妈也是身强力壮。阿星以为找一些在年龄、体格上相对较弱的就能获得胜利，想树起威风，却意外接连遭受打击。这正应和了中国的一句古语：人不可貌相。

（4）《如来神掌》：在传统作品里，拯救世界的领导者通常具有惊人的天赋和理性的判断力，并且在长期的艰苦奋斗中掌握了技能，而《功夫》中，江湖骗子用一本《如来神掌》就将"天下大任"交到乳臭未干的小阿星手中。当我们单纯地以为这是阿星小时候的一段被骗经历时，结果最终阿星真的练成了武功，并且用"如来神掌"打败了火云邪神，成了战胜邪恶势力的大英雄。一个个完全不合逻辑的想法在影片中出其不意地实现，造成落差，形成了荒诞的喜剧效果，此即"无厘头"喜剧。

"Mo lei tau" comes from the Cantonese phrase "mo lei tau gau", which literally means "cannot differentiate between head and tail of backbones", but is more commonly translated into slang as makes no sense, hard to understand, and nonsensical behaviors and talking. Stephen Chow excels at employing slang in his films, shaping a lot of eccentric icons with abnormal appearances, and reconstructing the existing figures and typical stories. Thereby a "mo lei tau" comedy style is established. In *Kung Fu Hustle*, several impressive clips display this comedy style:

(1) The cruel Axe Gang: at the beginning of the film, the distinctive Axe Gang dancing subverts spectators' expectations of the conventional ruthless and vicious gangsters portrayed in crime films, and also redefines the crime genre of films. On top of this, after Brother Sum, the leader of the Axe Gang, says "I don't kill women", viewers all believe that the wife of the boss of the Crocodile Gang could survive, but she is shot to death by the unexpected gunfire of Brother Sum. The dancing and massacre, the duplicity of "don't kill women", duplicity add a surprisingly hilarious appeal.

(2) The mysterious Fire Cloud Evil God: he is reportedly the world's most powerful martial artist, possessing extraordinary combat prowess, and the ultimate killer recruited by the Axe Gang at great expense. Despite his untidy appearance and status as a bald elderly man, not a wicked man, who wears glasses, undershirt, short pants, slippers and sitting on the toilet and reading a newspaper, there is a huge contrast between him and the image of the Fire Cloud Evil God, a master hand. Set in a weird and nervous atmosphere, his ordinary appearance enriches a humorous appeal. Moreover, the kung fu he mastered is the Toad Style. He can act like a toad and headbutt a person with immense force, which is created by computer special effects. Chinese kung fu generally pays attention to freehand brushwork, with more spiritual resemblance than physical resemblance. Here, the Toad Style is presented in a realistic animal form, and the exaggerated body performance creates a unique comedy effect.

(3) Sing's single fight: Sing first comes to the Pigsty Alley to extort, but failed.

Enraged by that, he tries to have a single fight with one of the residents in the alley. Firstly, he chooses a child, but is defeated by him unexpectedly. Then, he chooses a short man who actually is a giant man when he stands up. Eventually, he picks an elder woman, who is robust and strong. Sing thought that he could win by battling with someone who is relatively weak in age and physique, but he is wrong. As an old Chinese saying goes: Never judge people by their appearance.

(4) *Buddha's Palm*: Conventionally, the super heroes who save the world possess remarkable natural gift and rational judgement, and foster abilities in a long-term struggle. In *Kung Fu Hustle*, a shabby swindler sells the scroll of *Buddha's Palm* and transfers "the duty of upholding world peace" to little Sing. As the plot continues, audiences may believe that the little Sing is deceived, but Sing learns kung fu well, and uses Buddha's Palm to defeat the Fire Cloud Evil God. Eventually, Sing becomes the superhero to defeat evil forces. One by one completely illogical ideas are realized unexpectedly in the film, causing gaps and forming an absurd comic effect, which is "mo lei tau" comedy.

【"草根"人物】 Grassroots

草根文化指的是"平民文化""底层文化"。影片中，主要人物并不是黑帮，而是住在猪笼城寨的底层平民。贫民窟麻雀虽小，五脏俱全，在杂乱中显示出浓厚的生活气息，展现了底层人民的生活百态，既通俗，又不庸俗。影片中，有许多隐藏在民间的武林高手，他们以包租婆、包租公、苦力工人、裁缝、油炸小贩等普通劳动人民的形象出现。他们本来可以隐姓埋名过普通人的日子，却为了保护猪笼城寨的居民们而牺牲自己。影片中还有典型的"丑态"配角，比如大喊"包租婆，没水了"的酱爆，还有龅牙妹，强化了喜剧效果。周星驰电影中的配角往往是点睛之笔，尽管他们其貌不扬、身份平凡，但是拥有真诚善良、正直勇敢的美德。周星驰扮演的主角阿星，小时候受人欺负，也是草根阶层的代表。

Grassroot culture refers to the "ordinary culture" and the "culture of lower class". The protagonists depicted in the film are grassroots living in the Pigsty Alley, rather than gangsters. The slum covers a quite small area, but forms a highly populated community where tenants live in a messy environment. It tells stories of all walks of grassroots' life, realistic but not vulgar. Many of them, ordinary manual laborers, are actually masters concealing their identities, including landlady, landlord, coolie, dressmaker, and fried hawker. They could have lived the lives of ordinary people incognito, but sacrifice themselves to protect the residents of the Pigsty Alley. The film also portrayed some typical supporting characters shabbily dressed, such as Jiangbao who shouts, "Landlady! What happened to the water?" and rabbit-tooth Jane, which adds a comic effect. They are normal people without good looks, though they boast the virtues of sincerity, kindness, integrity and courage. Sing acted by Stephen Chow, who was bullied when he was little, is also the representative of the grassroots.

【海外影响】Global effect

中国的功夫片和武侠电影极具东方特色，成龙、李连杰等香港武打明星在华语电影圈乃至全球都具有一定知名度。《功夫》借助哥伦比亚电影公司便利的全球网络平台，在北美、欧洲、亚洲等56个以上的国家和地区进行全球分期放映，全球票房收入高达1.2亿美元，喜剧明星周星驰成功地掀起了全球功夫片的热潮。除了票房上的成功，《功夫》还获得了诸多国际电影节的青睐，得到了第63届美国电影金球奖最佳外语片奖提名、美国广播电视协会最佳外语片、《时代》杂志推荐的2005年全球十佳影片之一、阿姆斯特丹奇幻电影节银奖等多项荣誉。

Chinese martial arts films feature numerous martial arts combats between characters. Hong Kong martial arts stars such as Jackie Chan and Jet Li are well-known in the Chinese film circle and even around the world. Promoted by the global network platform provided by the Columbia Pictures Industries, Inc., *Kung Fu Hustle* had been simultaneously released in over 56 countries and regions covering North America, Europe and Asia, grossing 120 million dollars globally at the box office. Obviously, the comedy star Stephen Chow successively unveiled the gold rash of martial arts films. Aside from the great appeal at the box office, *Kung Fu Hustle* also gained recognition and awards at many international film festivals. It won the nomination of Best Foreign Language Film at the 63rd Golden Globe Awards, Best Foreign-Language Film of the Broadcast Film Critics Association, one of the top 10 Best Films in the world in 2005 as recommended by *Time* magazine, and the Silver Scream Award at the Amsterdam Fantastic Film Festival.

【经典配乐】Classical scores

影片《功夫》使用了多首经典配乐，导演周星驰亲自参与了本片的配乐工作。《功夫》的配乐将中西文化纳入其中，在原有喜剧性的基础上加入中国民族音乐和西方经典音乐，收到了东西融合的独特艺术效果，既有东方武侠的神韵，又有西方音乐的悠扬。

A plethora of classic scores is adopted in *Kung Fu Hustle*, and director Stephen Chow assisted in music design as well. With the integration of Chinese folk music and Western classic music, the film keeps the comic effect and allows spectators to witness the errantry spirit of Chinese masters and to enjoy the melodious western music.

1. 中国民族音乐 Chinese folk music

（1）《东海渔歌》：1959 年由马圣龙、顾冠仁所编的民乐合奏曲，旋律动听，朗朗上口，歌曲的内容主要是展示渔民们的辛苦劳作，在本片中主要表现猪笼城寨居民们生活的场景，为之后猪笼城寨的劫难作了铺垫。

（2）《将军令》：原为四川一带民乐，扬琴演奏，用于表现古时军队出征时的宏伟壮观。在《功夫》中经过重新编曲，表现斧头帮和猪笼城寨三大高手打斗的场景，主要选用了原曲中节奏紧凑的部分，表现打斗的紧张感。

（3）《闯将令》：表现战场上将士舍生忘死的大无畏精神，乐曲气势恢宏，本片用在火云邪神与包租婆夫妇相见时的场景。

（4）《英雄们战胜了大渡河》：本是一首革命歌曲，以大合唱的形式表现中国人民解放军历经万难进军西藏的革命精神。在本片中改为民乐演奏，改编后用在火云邪神与包租婆夫妇打斗的场景。

（5）《小刀会组曲》：作于 1959 年，被《新龙门客栈》《九品芝麻官》《大话西游》等多部经典影片使用，运用了唢呐、琵琶、古筝等中国传统乐器，时而凄凉，时而悲壮。在《功夫》中用在斧头帮与阿星的决战中，带有浓烈的英雄主义色彩。

（6）《十面埋伏》：民间著名琵琶乐曲，节奏紧凑，如疾风骤雨般，具有强烈的震撼力。阿星第一次出场时便使用该曲，在不断昂扬的情绪里，猪笼城寨迎来紧张刺激的功夫较量。

（1）"Fisherman's Song of the East China Sea": is a folk music ensemble composed by

Ma Shenglong and Gu Guanren in 1959. The melody is pleasant and catchy, and the content of the song is mainly to show the hard work of the fishermen. It is employed to depict the peaceful neighborhood of the Pigsty Alley, which lays a foundation for the untold misery happening in the alley.

(2) "Decree of the Sichuan General": is a folk music song/tune in Sichuan, and performed by dulcimer to depict the grandeur of the ancient armies when it went on an expedition. The soundtrack to the film *Kung Fu Hustle* is an arrangement to express the agitated battle between three masters of the Pigsty Alley and the Axe Gang.

(3) "Daring General": is to express the spirit of boldness and fearlessness of soldiers who disregard their own safety in the battlefields. The song is magnificent and used in the scene where the Fire Cloud Evil God meets the Landlord couple.

(4) "Heroes Conquer the Dadu River": is a revolutionary song, performed in the form of a cantata to honor the revolutionary spirit of the Chinese People's Liberation Army to march into Xizang after all difficulties. The music of the song is rearranged for the folk music to present the thrilling fight between the Fire Cloud Evil God and the Landlord couple.

(5) "Overture of the Dagger Society Suite": is composed in 1959 and adopted in many classical movies, namely, *New Dragon Gate Inn*, *Hail the Judge*, and *A Chinese Odyssey*, etc. With the performance of traditional Chinese instruments, such as Suona, Pipa and Guzheng, the changing gloomy, solemn and stirring mood is set. The score displays the Sing's great heroism when he has the decisive battle with the Axe Gang.

(6) "Ambush from Ten Sides": is a classical folk piece written for the Pipa. Changes in dynamic are brought into full play in this piece that produces a majestic narrative and a sense of agitation. Sing first appears with the score. In the constant excitable mood, the Pigsty Alley ushers in a tense and exciting kung fu contest.

2. 西方经典音乐 Western classic music

（1）《流浪者之歌》：西班牙小提琴曲，主要表现吉卜赛人的生活情趣。其中快板的部分为影片带来了诙谐幽默的效果，其歌谣的部分用于表现阿星悲痛的心情。

（2）《马刀舞曲》：芭蕾舞剧《加雅涅》中的群舞舞曲，用于表现人物彪悍、敏捷的特征。本片中将这首配乐用在阿星去精神病院营救火云邪神的场景。

（1）"Zigeunerweisen"：is a musical composition for violin in the Kingdom of Spain. The work expresses the life interest of the gypsies. In *Kung Fu Hustle*，its allegro parts add a humorous appeal，while its moderato suggests the negative mood of Sing.

（2）"Sabre Dance"：is a group dance music in the ballet "Gayane" for depicting valiant and acute characteristics. In *Kung Fu Hustle*，its use displays the scene where Sing goes to the mental hospital to rescue The Beast.

互动讨论 Interactive discussion

1. 结合剧情和老师的讲解，试着讲讲你对这几句话的理解。

Discuss your understanding of the following questions after learning about the plot and the teacher's explanation.

（1）火云邪神：天下武功，无坚不破，唯快不破。

The Fire Cloud Evil God：In the world of kung fu，speed defines the winner.

（2）阿星：不记得了也好，忘却也是一种幸福。

Sing：Memories can be painful. To forget may be a blessing.

2. 回答以下问题，并进行讨论。

Answer the following questions and have a discussion.

（1）你认为阿星是不是真正的英雄？为什么？

Do you think Sing is a real hero？Why？

（2）你还看过其他周星驰导演或者主演的电影吗？你最喜欢哪一部？

Have you watched other films directed by or starring Stephen Chow？Which one do you like best？

三、延伸阅读 Extended reading

中国香港，全称为"中华人民共和国香港特别行政区"，一般简称为"香港""港"。香港位于中国南部，北接深圳，南临南海。香港陆地部分占地 1 106.66 平方千米，主要分为三个部分：香港岛、九龙、"新界"，设有观塘区、荃湾区、深水埗区、沙田区等十八个区。中国香港在"二战"以后经济发展迅速，已经成为全球第三大金融中心，也是国际著名的自由港，与新加坡、韩国、中国台湾合称为"亚洲四小龙"。中国香港是一座经济、文化高度发达，兼具中西方文化特色的国际化大都市。

Hong Kong, China, officially "the Hong Kong Special Administrative Region of the People's Republic of China", is referred to "Hong Kong SAR" or "HKSAR" for short. It is located to the south of China, with neighboring Shenzhen in the north and the South China Sea in the south. The land area's 1,106.66 square kilometers consists of Hong Kong Island, the Kowloon Peninsula, the New Territories, with 18 districts, such as Kwun Tong District, Tsuen Wan District, Sham Shui Po District, and Sha Tin District. Since World War Ⅱ, the economy of Hong Kong has achieved rapid development to fuel Hong Kong's growth as the world's 3rd largest financial hub. It is also an internationally renowned free port. Together with Singapore, the Republic of Korea and Taiwan, China, it is known as the "Four Asian Tigers" for its developed economic level. Hong Kong, China, is an international metropolis with a highly developed economy and enriching culture, with both Chinese and western cultural characteristics.

历史 history

香港自先秦时期起就是中国的领土。1842 年 8 月，清政府在与英国战败以后签订了《南京条约》，将香港岛割让给英国。1860 年 10 月，又在《北京条约》中将九龙半岛界限街以南割让给英国。1898 年 6 月，英国又与清朝政府签订了《展拓香港界址专条》（"新界租约"），以租借为名占领了九龙半岛界限街以北、深圳河以南的地区，以及香港周边 200 多个大小岛屿，在合约中规定了租期为 99 年，即以 1997 年 6 月 30 日为结束日期。

Hong Kong has been China's territory since the Pre-Qin Period. In August 1842, the Qing Dynasty of China ceded Hong Kong Island to Britain after the First Opium War in accordance with the "Treaty of Nanking". In October 1860, the "Convention of Peking" stipulated that China was to cede the part of Kowloon Peninsula south to Britain. In June 1898, the "Convention for the Extension of Hong Kong Territory between the Qing Dynasty of China and the United Kingdom" ("New Territory Treaty") was signed. Under the convention the territories north of what is now Boundary Street and south of the Sham Chun River, and the surrounding over 200 islands, were leased to the United Kingdom for 99 years rent-free, expiring on 30 June 1997.

回归 Handover

1984 年，中国就香港问题与英国签订协议，两国约定 1997 年 7 月 1 日香港回归中国。在对香港的态度上，中国在坚持"一个中国"的原则下，承诺实行"一国两制"制度，即在香港设立特别行政区，保留香港原有的资本主义制度。1997 年 7 月 1 日，在盛大的回归典礼后，中国政府恢复对香港行使主权。1998 年，香港在中国政府的支持下度过亚洲金融危机。

In 1984，the British and the Chinese signed a formal agreement approving the handover of the island on July 1，1997，with China pledging to preserve existing structures of Hong Kong's capitalist system under a principle of "One Country，Two Systems". Thus，Hong Kong became China's first special administrative region. On July 1，1997，Hong Kong was peaceably handed over to China in a ceremony at which the Chinese government formally resumed the exercise of sovereignty over Hong Kong. In 1998，backed by the Chinese government，Hong Kong survived the Asian financial crisis.

粤语 Cantonese

又称"白话"，是广东一带流行的方言，也是中国七大方言之一。在广东、香港、澳门、广西东南部、东南亚部分地区及海外华人群体中使用较为广泛。粤语保留了较多的古汉语特征，并且具有完整的文字体系。粤语有九声六调，其发音具有韵律美。

Cantonese，also known as "vernacular"，is a popular dialect in Guangdong，and one of the seven varieties of Chinese dialects. Cantonese are frequently spoken by people in Guangdong，Hong Kong，Macao，the southeast Guangxi，countries and regions in Southeast Asia，and by groups of overseas Chinese. It has kept plenty of characteristics of ancient Chinese，and formed a complete system of its own characters. It has nine tones and six tone pitches that interact in complex ways，and its pronunciation sounds like poems with rhythm.

美食 Tastes

中国香港拥有"世界美食博览会"的美称，不但融合了中国、日本、新加坡、泰国等多个国家的美食风味，还有许多地道小吃在全国各地大受欢迎。香港的特色小吃有咖喱鱼蛋、菠萝包、鸡蛋仔、车仔面、云吞面等，特色甜品有杨枝甘露、港式奶茶等。香港的辣炒螃蟹、烧鹅腊味也非常有名。周星驰的电影《食神》，以及由徐克导演、著名影星张国荣主演的《金玉满堂》（1995 年），都对香港的美食文化有所展现。

Hong Kong, China is known as the "World's Food Fair". Here, you can taste different flavors from Japan, Singapore, and Thailand, etc. and varying local tastes, which are popular nationwide, such as curry fish balls, pineapple bread, egg waffle, HK boy cart noodles, wonton noodles, special desserts like mango pomelo sago and Hong Kong-style milk tea, etc. Moreover, fried spicy crabs, roast goose and cured meat in Hong Kong are well-known. Some movies, like *The God of Cookery* directed by Stephen Chow and *The Chinese Feast* (1995) produced by Tsui Hark and acted by the celebrated star Leslie Cheung Kwok-wing present the food culture of Hong Kong.

著名景点 Famous scenic spots

香港是著名的旅游胜地，也是购物天堂。香港的景点有维多利亚港、星光大道、迪士尼乐园、海洋公园、太平山、黄大仙祠、青马大桥、铜锣湾、中环、兰桂坊等。你可以吹着维多利亚港的晚风，看着夜景，在星光大道上和明星们的手印合影，去中环、兰桂坊感受都市的繁华，去铜锣湾购物，去旺角、尖沙咀感受经典港片里的场景，再去迪士尼乐园感受童话世界。香港虽小，值得玩的地方却很多。

Hong Kong is a famous tourist destination, as well as a shopping paradise. It boasts a lot of famous scenic spots, namely, Victoria Harbor, Avenue of Stars, Disneyland, Ocean Park Hong Kong, Victoria Peak, Sik Sik Yuen Wong Tai Sin Temple, Tsing Ma Bridge, Causeway Bay, Central Hong Kong, and Lan Kwai Fong, etc. You can enjoy the evening breeze off Victoria Harbor, watch the night scene, take pictures with the handprints of stars on the Avenue of Stars, go to Central and Lan Kwai Fong to experience the prosperity of the city, go shopping in Causeway Bay, go to Mong Kok and Tsim Sha Tsui to experience the scenes in classic Hong Kong films, and go to Disneyland to experience the fairy tale world. Although Hong Kong is small, there are many places worth visiting.

香港电影 Hong Kong films

香港是著名的电影之都，被称为"东方好莱坞"。香港电影业历史悠久，香港本土出产的影片可以追溯到 1909 年由上海亚细亚电影公司拍摄的黑白短片《偷烧鸭》。最早的香港电影制片公司是 1913 年黎民伟和美国人布罗斯基合办的华美影片公司，其摄制了故事短片《庄子试妻》。黎民伟的妻子严珊珊饰演婢女，成为中国电影历史上第一位登上银幕的女演员。因为大陆电影人的加入，香港电影在 1949 年以后发展迅速，在 20 世纪 70 年代更是迎来了发展高潮，以邵氏电影公司为代表的制片公司崛起，将香港的功夫片、都市片输出到东南亚，迅速占领了市场。二十世纪八九十年代是香港电影发展的黄金时期，香港的警匪片、武侠片、喜剧片、恐怖片、黑帮片等类型在全球占有重要位置，培养出了徐克、吴宇森、林超贤等著名导演，以及成龙、李连杰、张曼玉、刘德华等明星。

Hong Kong is a famous filmmaking hub, and touted as "Chinese Hollywood". Hong Kong film industry has a long history, with the first film traced back to the black-and-white short film, *Stealing a Roast Duck*, shot by the Asia Film Company in 1909. In 1913, American Benjamin Brosky and Chinese Li Minwei co-founded HK's first film studio, the Huamei (Chinese-American) Studio. The company shot the short drama film *Chuang Tzu Tests His Wife*. Li Minwei's wife Yan Shanshan played a servant girl, thus making her the first ever Chinese film actress. With the involvement of film workers from the mainland, the Hong Kong film has gained rapid development since 1949, and attained its apex in the 1970s. Filmmakers represented by the Shaw Brothers Ltd. have risen, exporting Hong Kong's kung fu films and urban films to Southeast Asia, and quickly dominating the market. The golden age of Hong Kong cinema was the 1980s – 1990s. Hong Kong's crime films, martial arts films, comedy films, horror films, gangster films and other genres occupy an important position in the world, and famous directors such as Tsui Hark, John Woo, and Dante Lam have emerged, as well as Jackie Chan, Jet Li, Maggie Cheung, Andy Lau and other stars.

CEPA 协议 CEPA

CEPA 即 Closer Economic Partnership Arrangement 的缩写，中文名称为《关于建立更紧密经贸关系的安排》。2003 年，中国内地与香港特别行政区签订了该协议，减少或免除关税，促进两地的贸易和经济，该协议促进了中国经济一体化的进程。进入 21 世纪，面对好莱坞大片的冲击和中国电影的崛起，香港电影在自身创新不足、市场萎缩的情况下面临着衰退的局面。CEPA 协议对于香港电影设置了一系列的扶持政策，其中包括 2004 年后生产的港产片将不再受到中国内地每年 20 部引进电影的限制。此外，有一定内地演职人员和投资的香港电影可以作为"合拍片"引进内地进行宣传和放映，不受进口配额的限制。内地庞大市场的支撑极大地促进了香港电影的恢复。电影《无间道Ⅲ：终极无间》是 CEPA 协议实施后第一部在内地上映的香港、内地合拍电影。陈可辛导演的《中国合伙人》（2013 年）、林超贤导演的《红海行动》（2018 年）、徐克的《狄仁杰》系列电影等均为合拍片。

CEPA is the abbreviation of Closer Economic Partnership Arrangement. It is translated as "关于建立更紧密经贸关系的安排" in Chinese. Closer Economic Partnership Arrangement （CEPA）is the first free trade agreement ever concluded by the Chinese mainland and Hong Kong. It was signed in 2003, aiming to reduce or eliminate tariffs, thereby to fuel trade and economy of both areas. CEPA agreement accelerates the process of Chinese economic integration. During the 21st century, amid the popularity of Hollywood films and the emergence of domestic films, the Hong Kong films lacked innovations and were subject to market recession. The CEPA agreement provided a window of supporting policies for Hong Kong film industry. It granted the Hong Kong films produced after 2004 access to the Mainland without restriction of China's annual quota of 20 imported films. In addition, the Hong Kong films invested and starred in by some investors and actors respectively from the Mainland can be imported to the Mainland to advertise and release as "cooperation films", without the limitation of import quota. To a large extent, the domestic huge market backs up the revitalization of the Hong Kong films. Since the launching of the CEPA agreement, the first cooperation film released in the Mainland was *Infernal Affairs* Ⅲ, followed *by American Dreams in China* （2013）directed by Peter Chan, *Operation Red Sea* （2018）produced by Dante Lam, and *Detective Dee*, the film series, made by Tsui Hark.

四、课后思考 After class thinking

1. 你看过香港电影吗？谈谈你对香港电影的印象。

Have you seen any Hong Kong films? Talk about your impression of Hong Kong films.

2. 观看了影片《功夫》之后，你对于中国功夫有怎样的认知？

After watching *Kung Fu Hustle*, what is your understanding of Chinese kung fu?

五、互动时间 Interaction time

一起来学习一些常用的粤语词组吧！

Let's learn some common Cantonese phrases together！

食饭＝吃饭 have a meal

揸车＝开车 drive a car

行啰＝走吧 go

老细你好＝老板你好 hello，boss

你虾我＝你欺负我 you bully me

你咪理＝你不要管 leave alone

你喺边？＝你在哪里？where are you？

我好挂住你＝我很想念你 I miss you so much

我唔识得你＝我不认识你 I don't know you

我唔系故意的＝我不是故意的 I didn't mean it

第十单元
刺杀小说家

本单元重点

1.了解电影《刺杀小说家》的基本情节
2.了解中国兵马俑的相关知识

本单元难点

1.分析电影《刺杀小说家》的艺术特色
2.了解中国秦朝的历史知识以便分析电影

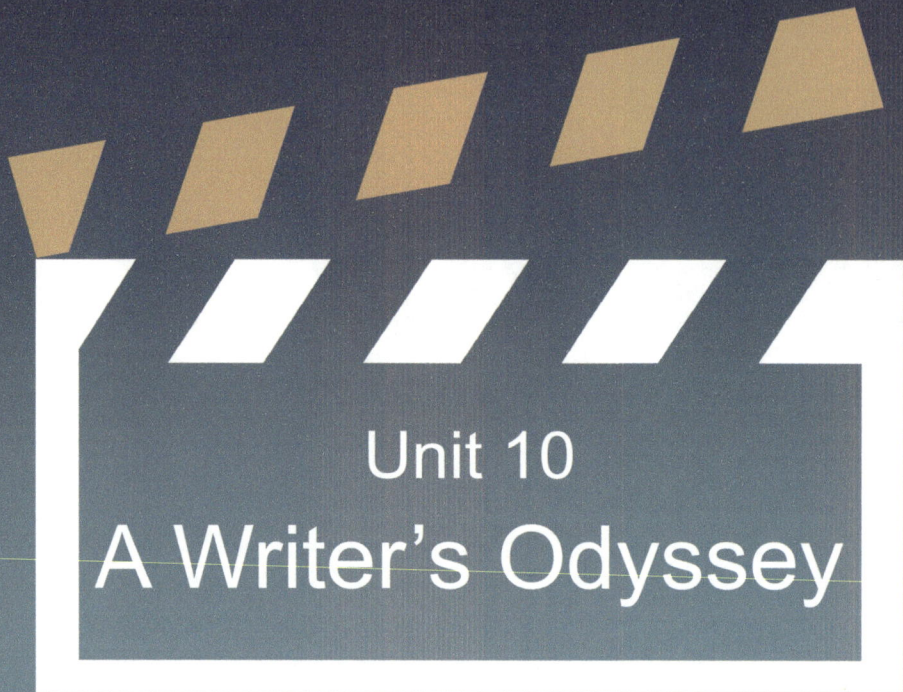

Unit 10
A Writer's Odyssey

🔊 **Key points**

1.Learn about the plots of *A Writer's Odyssey*
2.Learn about the relevant information on Terracotta Warriors

🔊 **Difficult points**

1.Analyze the artistic characteristics of *A Writer's Odyssey*
2.Learn about the history of the Qin Dynasty and understand the film well

《刺杀小说家》：只要相信，就能实现

A Writer's Odyssey：As Long as You Hold the Film Belief, All Wishes Will be Realized

一、丝路放映厅 Silk Road screen hall

导演：路阳

原著：双雪涛

编剧：陈舒/禹扬/秦海燕/路阳

主演：雷佳音/董子健/杨幂/于和伟/郭京飞

类型：奇幻/冒险

制片国家/地区：中国内地

上映日期：2021 – 02 – 12

片长：130 分钟

英文名：*A Writer's Odyssey*

Director：Lu Yang

Story writer：Shuang Xuetao

Screenwriter：Chen Shu/Yu Yang/Qin Haiyan/Lu Yang

Starring：Lei Jiayin/Dong Zijian/Yang Mi/Yu Hewei/Guo Jingfei

Type：Fantasy/Adventure

Production country/region：Chinese mainland

Release date：February 12，2021

Length：130 minutes

English name：*A Writer's Odyssey*

剧情梗概 Plot synopsis

影片根据双雪涛同名小说改编，故事讲述了丢失女孩的中年男人关宁在寻找女儿下落时被阿拉丁集团相中，让他去刺杀小说《弑神》的作者路空文，原因是小说《弑神》中"赤发鬼"的走向影响着集团老总李沐的健康，在刺杀任务快要完成时，关宁突然发现小说中的女孩与女儿同名且相似，为救"女儿"，关宁放弃了自杀，并帮助小说家完成"弑神"。

This film is an adaptation of a literary work with the same title written by Shuang Xuetao. Middle-aged Guan Ning, whose daughter was lost, was chosen and contracted to assassinate the novelist Lu Kongwen by the Aladdin Group when he tried to search his girl. That's because the Chairperson Li Mu's health was affected by the "Redmane", the character of the novel *God Slayer* written by Lu Kongwen. When the assassination mission was about to be completed, Guan Ning surprisingly knew that the little girl, a character of the novel, was similar to his lost daughter. To save his daughter by saving the little girl, he did not commit suicide but instead helped the novelist "slay a deity".

重点词汇 Important vocabularies

寻找	xúnzhǎo	*v.*	search for
集团	jítuán	*n.*	group
健康	jiànkāng	*n.*	health
任务	rènwù	*n.*	mission
相似	xiāngsì	*adj.*	similar
自杀	zìshā	*v.*	suicide

例句 Example sentences

1. 关宁花费了六年的时间还在寻找女儿的踪迹。

Guan Ning had been searching for any clue of his daughter for six years.

2. 阿拉丁集团的幕后老板是李沐。

The chairperson of the Aladdin Group is Li Mu.

3. 保持愉悦的心情，有助于身体健康。

Keeping a good attitude is good for body health.

4. 理清思路有利于我们高效地完成任务。

Clearing our minds helps us finish the mission effectively.

5. 世界上或许还有另外一个人，和你有着相似的容貌。

Maybe there is someone who is similar to you in appearance.

6. 警察在浴室发现了自杀的女孩，满地都是鲜血。

The police found the girl who committed suicide in the bathroom, covered with blood.

语言练习 Language practices

请为以下句子选择合适的词语进行填空。

Please fill in the blanks with the appropriate words for the following sentences.

1. 吸烟不利于身体（　　　　）。

Smoking is not good for people's （　　　　）.

2. 淘宝是阿里巴巴（　　　　）旗下的公司。

Taobao is owned by the Alibaba （　　　　）.

3. 为了（　　　　）到杀人的真凶，大家已经两个晚上没有休息了。

To （　　　　） for the killer, nobody had any sleep for two days.

4. 有些人因遭遇不幸而（　　　　），实在令人惋惜。

It is regrettable that someone （　　　　） themselves because of misfortune.

5. 爸爸的眼睛和女儿的眼睛极为（　　　　）。

The daughter's eyes are very （　　　　） to her father's.

6. 读完一本书的首要（　　　　）是做一个思维导图。

The first （　　　　） when you finished a book is to make a mind map.

二、丝路大讲堂 Silk Road lecture hall

【导演特色】Featuring director

路阳，1979 年出生于北京，2007 年毕业于北京电影学院导演系，中国内地男导演、编剧、自由酷鲸影业董事。2010 年，凭借导演电影处女作《盲人电影院》，获得中国金鸡电影节最佳导演处女作奖、韩国釜山国际电影节新浪潮单元 KNN 奖、俄罗斯喀山电影节最佳影片奖。2012 年，完成的第二部电影《房车奇遇》入围韩国釜山国际电影节"亚洲之窗单元"。2014 年 8 月 7 日，执导的个人第三部电影作品《绣春刀》

上映，并因此获得第 16 届华鼎奖最佳新锐导演称号。同年成立自由酷鲸影业，公司及分公司现有近百人。2017 年 7 月，执导的个人第四部电影《绣春刀：修罗战场》上映。2021 年 2 月 12 日，执导的电影《刺杀小说家》上映。2021 年 4 月，担任电视剧《风起陇西》导演。

Lu Yang, born in Beijing in 1979, is a male director, screenwriter and a board member of Free Whale Film Inc. He graduated from the Department of Directing of the Beijing Film Academy in 2007. In 2010, he directed his debut film *My Spectacular Theatre*, which earned him the Best Director of the Debut Award at the 28th Golden Rooster Awards and won the KNN Award at the 15th Busan International Film Festival and the Best Picture Award at the Kazan International Muslim Film Festival. In 2012, his second film *Ex Fighting* was selected in "A Window on Asian films" of the 17th Busan International Film Festival. His third historical action film *Brotherhood of Blades* was released on August 7, 2014, for which he received Young Director of the Year Award at the China Film Director Association, and Best Director of the Debut Award at the 16th Huading Awards. In the same year, he founded Free Whale Film Inc. which has nearly one hundred employees. In July 2017, his fourth film *Brotherhood of Blades Ⅱ: The Infernal Battlefield*, was released. On February 12, 2021, *A Writer's Odyssey* was released. In April 2021, he directed the TV series, *The Wind Blows from Longxi*.

【空间作用】Space form

路阳导演在影片《刺杀小说家》中继承了以往浪漫化意象表达与想象和现实高度重叠的影像叙事手段，并以游戏叙事来综合影像元素，小说式的套层结构实现了幻想与现实两个世界之间的沟通转换。在本片中，现实世界与小说世界迥然不同，现实世界有着可以指认的空间——重庆，小说家路空文操控的重庆方言使得真实感得以强化，而小说世界完全是虚拟的皇城，使用全景镜头与俯视镜头进行拍摄，并时刻紧跟人物的脚步，使电影更加接近第三人称的游戏视角，观众仿佛游戏玩家，增强了对角色的形象投射与对电影空间的沉浸感。

The director Lu Yang follows his romantic and imaginative style to establish a film with the integration of reality and virtuality. And with that, he obtains inspirations from video games to make feature films more attractive. A story within a story, also referred to as an embedded narrative, is a literary device which allows the free transformation of the two worlds. In this film, the realistic world is totally different from the virtual world. Chongqing is a real existing space, and the novelist Lu Kongwen speaks in a Chongqing dialect to augment reality, while the novel world is a virtual imperial city, which uses panoramic lens and overhead lens to shoot and keep up with the footsteps of the characters, making the film closer to the third person perspective of the game. The audience is like a game player, enhancing the image projection of the characters and the immersion of the film space.

【时空穿越】 Time travel

本片的故事具有中国式风格的视觉奇观，涉及现实与虚拟两个时空。从"小说影响现实"的设定开始，观众不自觉地跟随镜头运转来回切换时空实现无缝衔接，而影片正是借助小说世界对现实世界进行自反性的思考，通过对善的共同信仰与观众再次建立起联系。全片充满奇幻化的人物造型，皇都十三坊并立和凡人弑神的异世界图景，为观众传递了富有新意的奇幻美学体验。

This film provides audiences a visual feast with Chinese style, with two interwoven worlds existing in parallel. The fantasy character images, abnormal visual establishments, like the thirteen districts in Dragon District and mortal god slayer broaden audiences' horizons. From the outset, audiences are attracted by the plot setting, travelling together with the actors in the different worlds. This special design aims to establish connections with the viewers and arouse their common belief in goodness.

【工业美学】 Industrial aesthetics

《刺杀小说家》这部影片是中国电影工业化进程中第一次完整使用虚拟拍摄技术的影片，将虚拟拍摄、动作捕捉、实拍、CG 等多项技术整合在一起，为观众呈现了一个充满想象力的东方异世界。影片恢宏大气且具中国古风的场景，配合奇异生物赤发鬼、红甲武士等令人眼花缭乱的打斗，体现了中国电影人打磨精品的职业道德和敬业精神。标准化的全新工业流程结合美学设计构建平行世界的创意框架，在路空文以小说改变现实的人物设置下，使得小说世界作为现实世界的镜像而存在。

A *Writer's Odyssey* is the first film completely produced by virtual shooting in the Chinese film industry. It integrates virtual shooting, motion capture, real shooting, and CG（Computer Graphics）together, providing audiences with an astonishing visual experience and enriching their understanding of the mysterious eastern world, particularly the special effects of the Chinese ancient style, in the battle between Redmane and the crimson cavalrymen. The creative idea to build a parallel world was adopted under the standard but renewed film industry process, combined with aesthetic design. That makes sense for the novelist Lu Kongwen, whose fiction plots change the virtual world accordingly.

【北极熊与女儿】 Polar bear and daughter

在原小说中，主人公千兵卫执行"刺杀小说家"这一任务，是为了获得高额奖金去北极看北极熊。为什么一定要去看北极熊呢？在小说的结尾，千兵卫对小橘子说："我和你妈妈准备带你去看熊。很可爱的熊。"原来几年前，千兵卫的妻子弄丢了他们的女儿小橘子，失去至亲骨肉后，他将去北极看女儿最喜欢的北极熊作为释放情感的出口。影片中，与人物原型千兵卫相比，关宁的形象被塑造得更加丰满，一开场就上演了石头精准拦车的戏码。扔石头绝技为后面屠灵找到关宁，为救女儿去做刺杀任务作了合理解释。随着后续故事的展开，观众才意识到关宁这一角色已经不单是杀手，并且与小说世界有着密不可分的关系。

In the literary source, the main character Qian Bingwei was hired to murder the novelist for a great monetary reward. Then he could go to see the polar bears at the North pole. But he was not doing it for himself. At the ending of the novel, Qian Bingwei told Tangerine, "Mama and I wish to take you to see polar bears. They are very cute." A few years previously, the wife of Qian Bingwei lost their daughter Tangerine accidently. After that, Qian Bingwei's unfulfilled wish to take his daughter to see polar bears motivated him to be positive. In the film, Guan Ning, the leading actor, is more vivid than the prototype Qian Bingwei. He showed his unique skill, throwing stones precisely to stop a car at the start of the film. It offers a reasonable explanation for why Tu Ling came to him, and he accepted the murder contract. As the plot continues, audiences soon discover that Guan Ning was not only a killer, but involved in the virtual world as one of the characters.

【赤发鬼折树枝】Redmane broke branches gently

影片里赤发鬼在大战前夕折下树枝的动作被观众发现像极了佛拈花一笑。佛陀的"拈花一笑"旨在强调佛即禅。禅在于性，不被文字表象迷惑。故传禅宗之法，最好的方式是"以心传心"：心一念悟，则一念成佛；心一念迷，则万古不悟。赤发鬼虽被称为"佛母"，模仿佛的行为，可终究逃不过吞食生灵的贪念和恶行。

It is believed that the activity that Redmane breaks branches gently is similar to Mahakshyapa's understanding smile when Gautama Buddha showed a flower. The "Mahakshyapa's understanding smile when Gautama Buddha showed a flower" reflects that Buddhism is Zen. Zen emphasizes nature of mind, having one mind rather than trapped by texts. Therefore, the best way to popularize Zen thoughts is "having one mind". To acquire enlightenment, then is to become a Buddha; if not, then to be indulged. Although the Redmane is called "deity", imitating the behaviors of Buddha, he cannot escape the punishment for his greed and the evil of his massacre.

【平行世界】Parallel world

影片分为现实和小说虚幻世界两条平行线，相互联系，同步变化，一一对应。现实世界围绕男主关宁（父亲）找女儿小橘子展开，小说世界围绕路空文（男孩）找赤发鬼推进，在现实世界男主关宁与小说家路空文的相处中，新的灵感促使小说世界一点点发生变化，从男主关宁得知女儿已死的真相到小说家一事无成放弃生命开始，小说世界里与女儿同名且相似的小橘子还活着的假想成了男主关宁的精神寄托。随着故事的发展，男主关宁与小说家（路空文）在现实世界联手对抗李沐的刺杀，小说虚拟世界里，关宁作为红甲武士，听到女儿的笛声后与路空文并肩作战，消灭了赤发鬼，成功完成"弑神"。

There is a realistic world and a virtual world created in the novel in this film. Both connect closely with synchronal change. In the realistic world, storyline number one follows the leading actor Guan Ning (father) who tries to find his daughter Tangerine. While in the virtual world, story number two follows Lu Kongwen (boy) who determines to battle with Redmane for revenge. Following along with Guan Ning in the realistic world, the novelist Lu Kongwen sparkles inspirations constantly, making the virtual world change as well. Guan

Ning is grieved when he discovered the truth that his daughter was dead，and the novelist wants to commit suicide for his failure．But suddenly，Guan Ning stops pitying himself and has an expectation that his daughter may still be alive soon after he found that there was a character similar to his daughter in the novel，whose name is Tangerine too．As the plot develops，Guan Ning and the novelist（Lu Kongwen）together fight against the murderer of Li Mu in the realistic world．While in the virtual world，Guan Ning as the crimson cavalryman who is awakened by his daughter's tune，joins together to fight with Lu Kongwen（boy）to defeat Redmane，thus "a deity is slain"．

平行世界人物对应关系

现实世界	小说虚拟世界
路空文（小说家）	路空文（男孩）
关宁	红甲武士
李沐（老总）	赤发鬼
小橘子（关宁的女儿）	小橘子（白翰坊的小女孩）
屠灵	黑甲
流浪小男孩	小橘子哥哥
人贩子	暴徒

Characters

Realistic World	Virtual World
Lu Kongwen（novelist）	Lu Kongwen（a boy）
Guan Ning	Crimson Cavalryman
Li Mu（chairperson）	Redmane
Tangerine（Guan Ning's daughter）	Tangerine（a girl in Baihan district）
Tu Ling	One-eyed monster
Homeless boy	Tangerine's brother
Human smugglers	Gangsters

【《弑神》】 *God Slayer*
小说《弑神》中有一则有关赤发鬼与久天的传说，赤发鬼与久天是共患难的兄弟，

在助帝王成就霸业后，赤发鬼篡夺了皇位，而久天则死在赤发鬼之手。可当看到赤发鬼的真容之后，观众可以发现赤发鬼根本就不是人，那他与久天的关系究竟是什么呢？当年久天利用赤发鬼的能力，帮助帝王完成了霸业后，因无法掌控赤发鬼，最终酿成了玩火者必自焚的惨剧。而赤发鬼额头上的那把剑，则为久天最后的呐喊作了见证。影片中路空文与独眼怪的经历或许正是历史的重现，独眼怪以吸附宿主的血液为生，而它之所以会听从路空文的命令，是因为它的道行只有四百年，无法与赤发鬼相提并论，此时的独眼怪与路空文不正像年轻时的久天与赤发鬼吗？

A story of Redmane and Jiutian is mentioned in the novel *God Slayer*. Jiutian is the sworn brother of Redmane. After they helped the king to be crowned, Redmane usurped the power and killed Jiutian. It seems that Redmane was not a human after seeing his face. What's the relationship between them? In the past, Jiutian took advantage of Redmane's capability to help enthrone the king, but he could not control Redmane and died. The sword struck in Redmane eyebrow symbols the last effort to defeat Redmane. As for Lu Kongwen and the one-eyed monster, it relies on Lu Kongwen's blood, while Lu Kongwen needs his power to kill Redmane. Isn't the one-eyed monster and Lu Kongwen the same as Jiutian and Redmane when they were young?

【世界电影中那些关于平行世界的故事】Similar films

（1）《土拨鼠之日》：是哈罗德雷米斯执导的作品，1993 年在美国上映，该片主要讲述了主人公菲尔执行任务偶遇暴风雪后时间被定格，始终停留在报道土拨鼠日的那一天，直到打动女主人公后共度良宵，永无休止的土拨鼠日才终于过去。

（2）《时空恋旅人》：于 2013 年上映，是一部浪漫的英国喜剧。男主人公遗传了家族穿越时空的超能力，于是他试图穿越回到过去，改变自己的命运。

（3）《蝴蝶效应》：2004 年上映的由埃里克·布雷斯、J. 麦凯伊·格鲁伯执导的科幻惊悚电影，讲述了 20 岁的大学生伊万在小时候经历了一系列糟糕的事情，损坏了他原本完美的人生。在童年可怕记忆的折磨下，伊万请求心理医生的帮助，医生鼓励他把发生的事情一件件详细记下来，在一点一点的记录中找回了孩童时期的记忆，但是事情远远没有结束。

（4）《恐怖游轮》：2009 年上映的一部心理悬疑影片，讲述的是单身母亲杰西和一群朋友乘坐游艇出海游玩遇到风暴，登上经过的一艘游轮后却发现这艘 1930 年失踪的神秘游轮里空无一人，随之而来的连环凶杀让杰西等人陷入轮回的恐怖之中。

（1）*Groundhog Day*：is a work directed by Harold Remis. It is released in the United States in 1993. The film mainly tells that the hero Phil is frozen after encountering a snowstorm when he is performing a task. He always stays on the day of reporting Groundhog Day until he moves the heroine and spends a good night together. The endless Groundhog Day finally passed.

（2）*About Time*：is a British romantic comedy film released in 2013. The film is about a young man Tim with the ability to time travel who tries to change his past in hopes of improving his future.

（3）*The Butterfly Effect*：is a 2004 American science fiction thriller film written and directed by Eric Bress and J. Mackye Gruber. A 20-year-old college student Evan Treborn, who experiences blackouts and memory loss throughout his childhood, lives a different life. Later, he requires a doctor to help him escape the torment of his horrible childhood. The doctor encourages him to document everything that happened at that time in detail. By doing this, Evan recovers the lost memory, but there are unintended consequences for all.

（4）*Triangle*：is a 2009 psychological horror film. The film is about a single mother Jess who goes on a boating trip with several friends. When they are forced to abandon their ship due to storm, they board an ocean liner as it passes. But they find that no one is onboard and that the ship went missing in 1930. An endless loop of serial murders terrorizes them.

互动讨论 Interactive discussion

结合剧情，谈谈你对以下问题的理解。

Discuss your understanding of the following questions after learning about the plot.

1. 影片中，你最喜欢哪一个角色人物？为什么？

What's your favorite character in this film? why?

2. 平行世界的电影吸引你吗？你还知道哪些平行世界的故事？

Do you like the movie designed with the concept of parallel worlds? Do you know anything about it?

3. 为什么人类要"弑神"？你认为"弑神"代表着什么呢？

Why would a human try to "slay a deity"? What's your opinion?

三、延伸阅读 Extended reading

1.《山海经》 *The Classic of Mountains and Rivers*

《山海经》作为一部我国古老的奇书，记载了各种脍炙人口的神话传说。它不仅记载了大量的民间传说中的地理知识，还记载了上古人们的创造发明和实践活动，具有非凡的文献价值，对中国古代历史、地理、文化、中外交通、民俗、神话等研究均有参考。

重要的是，《山海经》呈现的神奇瑰丽、大气恢宏、脑洞大开的想象世界，开启了先人思维模式的转变，可以说，它对后世文学、艺术等各方面的创作都产生了深远的影响。现在大多数学者认为，《山海经》是一部早期有价值的地理著作。

The Classic of Mountains and Rivers is a Chinese classic text as well as a collection of Chinese mythology. It records a lot of geographical knowledge in folklore. On top of this, creative inventions and practical activities of ancient people are recorded in this book. It is an important record of Chinese history, geography, culture, transportation at home and abroad, folklore and methodology.

More importantly, the imaginary world in this masterpiece enables the transform of thinking, and has made a profound impact on creative works, such as literature and art. Some great minds have given high praise to it. Today, most scholars believe that it is a valuable geographical work in ancient times.

相关纪录片 Relevant documentary

2011 年，央视栏目首播《失落的天书·山海经》，分上下两集，全长 53 分钟，讲述了 2007 年 7 月吉林市的宋先生早晨起床洗漱时，发现了一个身似龟、嘴似鹰、背似恐龙的怪物，从事古文化研究的宫玉海证实其为多旋龟，北京市玉石收藏家任楠和北京石刻艺术博物馆刘卫东研究一块古玉时发现了一些疑似微生物和时隐时现的珠子状微生物等，由此介绍了奇书《山海经》和书中很多不为人知的上古时代的生物。

"The Classic of Mountains and Seas: Great Masterpiece", made by CCTV (China Central Television) and released in 2011, was filmed in two episodes with a run time of 53 minutes each. Its first episode documents the unexpected discovery of Mr. Song in Jilin Province of China throughout July 2007. When he gets up and washes up in the morning, he finds a monster with a body like turtle, a mouth like eagle, a back like dinosaur. An expert Gong Yuhai studying ancient cultures confirms that the creature is a black tortoise. And the jade collector Ren Nan from Beijing and Liu Weidong, an expert of the Beijing Stone Carving Art Museum, observes that some suspected bead-shaped microorganism when he studied an ancient jade. Some unknown beasts described in *The Classic of Mountains and Seas* and the book itself are introduced.

2. 作家双雪涛 Shuang Xuetao（the author of the literary source）

双雪涛，中国当代作家，1983 年 9 月 8 日出生于辽宁沈阳，毕业于吉林大学。2011 年以小说处女作《翅鬼》获首届华文世界电影小说奖首奖，先后出版小说集《平原上的摩西》《飞行家》。2017 年 4 月，获第十五届华语文学传媒大奖 "年度最具潜力新人" 称号。2018 年 5 月，凭借小说《北方化为乌有》获首届汪曾祺华语小说奖短篇小说奖。2020 年 10 月，以作品《猎人》获第三届宝珀理想国文学奖。在人物刻画上，双雪涛经常采用极简的白描式手法，脱离诗意化的表达，语言叙述表层对人物外貌的美化被剥离。

Shuang Xuetao was born in Shenyang City, Liaoning Province on September 8, 1983, and graduated from Jilin University. He is a famous contemporary Chinese writer. *The Slave With Wings* (2011), his debut novel, won the first prize at the 14th Taipei Literature Awards. *Moses on the Plain* and *The Aviator* were published successively. In April 2017, he won the 15th Chinese Literature Media Awards' Newcomer with the Best Potential. In May 2018, his novel *The North Disappeared* won the Short Story Award of the first Wang Zengqi Chinese Fiction Prize. In October 2020, *The Hunter* won the third Blancpain-Imaginist Literary Prize. He often uses common speech to depict a character, not poetically but emphasizing the nature of language.

影视改编 Film adaptation

双雪涛是一位东北新文学作家。2010 年，还在沈阳做银行职员的双雪涛写了第一部小说《翅鬼》，两年后辞职，专职写作。2015 年他离开东北，来到了北京。从 2016

年开始，双雪涛陆续出版了《天吾手记》《平原上的摩西》《聋哑时代》《飞行家》《猎人》等，成为当下中国最引人注目的青年作家之一，《平原上的摩西》的腰封上，形容他是"迟来的大师"。与此同时，他的小说在电影市场炙手可热，改编版权被各大影视公司争相购买，市场价值飙升，其作品陆续被搬上大银幕，包括《刺杀小说家》《平原上的摩西》。

Shuang Xuetao is a new Dongbei literature writer. He wrote his debut fiction *The Slave With Wings* in 2010 when he was employed in a bank. Two years later, he resigned and became a full-time author. In 2015, he relocated to Beijing from Dongbei. His works have been successively published from 2016, including *Tian Wu's Notes*, *Moses on the Plain*, *The Deaf-Mute Age*, *The Aviator*, and *The Hunter*. Thus, he has become one of the most popular young writers. The review of *Moses on the Plain* tells that he is a "promising master". Meanwhile, his fiction works are sought after by the major film makers and they are eager to buy film rights to his books. Some film adaptations have been released to the public, such as *A Writer's Odyssey* and *Moses on the Plain*.

《平原上的火焰》 *Fire on the Plain*

该片改编自双雪涛的小说《平原上的摩西》，讲述了由一起出租车司机被杀案揭开的陈年往事。新案旧案交错，展现了中国发展道路上给人们留下的烙印。原著风格鲜明，文化底蕴深厚，是极具市场吸引力的现实主义题材，涉及家庭、情感、时代变迁等多个话题层面，影片暂定于 2023 年上映。

The film based on a popular novel *Moses on the Plain* by writer Shuang Xuetao. It tells the story of a man（Liu）investigating the murder of a taxi driver. New cases and old cases are intertwined, showing the imprint left on people on the road of China's development. The original style is distinctive and culturally rich, and is a realistic subject with great market appeal, involving multiple topics such as family, emotions, and the changing times. The film is tentatively released in 2023.

四、课后思考 After class thinking

1. 你去过重庆吗？谈谈你对重庆的感受。

Have you been to Chongqing? How did you like it?

2. 电影中的赤发鬼是一个什么样的人物？你知道《山海经》记载了多少个神怪畏兽吗？

What's your understanding of Redmane? How many beasts can you recall from in *The Classic of Mountains and Seas*?

3. 在你的国家中，有没有传奇的故事？可以与同学们分享。

Are there any myths in your country? Share with your classmates.

五、互动时间 Interaction time

经典影视配音互动，并尝试与同伴用重庆方言说一说。

Watch the film and conduct dubbing practice in a Chongqing dialect with partners.

片段一：

大家好，我们继续讲我的小说。

书接上回，姐姐抓着刀杆支撑精疲力竭的身体，她抬头看到了空文。姐姐无力挤出一个笑容地："跑……往西……快……"

话音未落，姐姐被一只脚重重踩趴在地上，是那个行脚老僧，只见他右手一送，青色的长刀就刺进了姐姐的后背，姐姐的脸缓缓垂了下去。

在空文眼前，东北方向几百里开外，有什么东西在发光，空文望向远方，他看到了一座城，穿透云层的阳光客啬地笼罩着城，那座城宏大而又奇异，冉凉国的皇都——云中城。

就这一会儿，皇都深处禁宫中心的山顶上，赤发鬼好像感觉到了什么，少年的眼神坚毅了起来，他握紧了手中的薙刀。

与此同时，远在皇都山顶的赤发鬼突然感到头痛欲裂，是以前的旧伤，那伤口不知怎么就裂了开来，剧烈的头痛甚至让他高大的身躯倒了下去……

Part One：

Hello, everyone. Let's continue my novel.

The last time the book was picked up, the elder sister grabbed the knife bar to support her exhausted body. She looked up and saw Kongwen. The elder sister couldn't squeeze out a smile and said, "Run... West... Hurry..."

The elder sister was heavily trampled on the ground by one foot. It was the old monk who was a peddler. As soon as he gave it away with his right hand, the blue long knife stabbed her in the back, and her face slowly dropped.

In front of Kongwen, hundreds of miles away from the northeast, something was shining. Kongwen looked into the distance, and he saw a city. The sun penetrating the clouds was stingily enveloping the city. The city was grand and strange. The capital of Ranliang was Yunzhong City.

Just then, on the top of the mountain in the Forbidden City, the Redmane seemed to feel something. The young man's eyes were firm, and he clenched his knife.

At the same time, the Redmane, who was far away at the top of the mountain in the imperial capital, suddenly felt a headache. It was an old wound. The wound broke somehow. The severe headache even made his tall body fall down...

片段二：

少年空文下了神木峰走出狄山向皇都云中城进发，头二百里路很艰辛，空文徒步前进，直到在洛水边的渡口，他搭上了去皇都的货船。

洛水的怪浪和水兽，让空文心惊不已，好在不晕船，之后会如何空文不清楚，空文只知道要是不去找赤发鬼，活着便没有什么必要，这世上已经没有人在等他，除了那个叫作赤发鬼的人。

赤发鬼感觉到了空文的存在，想起了空文的父亲，那个曾经的朋友，也是曾经他唯一害怕的人。

也好，赤发鬼心里想反正老子也寂寞太久了……

Part Two：

The young man Kongwen got off the Shenmu Peak and went out of Dishan Mountain to the imperial capital Yunzhong City. The first 200 miles were very hard. Kongwen walked on foot until he got on the freighter to the imperial capital at the ferry near Luoshui.

The strange waves and water animals in Luoshui frightened Kongwen. Fortunately, he did not get seasick. Later, Kongwen was not clear. Kongwen only knew that if he did not find the Redmane, there would be no need to live. No one in the world was waiting for him, except the man called the Redmane.

The Redmane felt the existence of Kongwen, and thought of Kongwen's father, the former friend, and the only person he was afraid of.

Well, the Redmane thinks that I have been lonely for too long anyway...

参考文献

References

[1] 艾伦，戈梅里. 电影史：理论与实践 [M]. 最新修订版. 李迅，译. 北京：北京联合出版公司，2016.

[2] 巴赞. 电影是什么？[M]. 崔君衍，译. 北京：商务印书馆，2017.

[3] 波德维尔，汤普森. 电影艺术：形式与风格 [M]. 插图修订8版. 曾伟祯，译. 北京：北京联合出版公司，2015.

[4] 常修泽. 中国东北转型通论 [M]. 辽宁：辽宁人民出版社，2020.

[5] 戴锦华. 电影批评 [M]. 2版. 北京：北京大学出版社，2015.

[6] 范文澜. 中国通史简编 [M]. 上海：上海三联书店，2021.

[7] 韩茂莉. 中国历史地理十五讲 [M]. 北京：北京大学出版社，2015.

[8] 黄仁宇. 中国大历史 [M]. 北京：生活·读书·新知三联书店，2008.

[9] 贾内梯. 认识电影 [M]. 插图11版. 伯格曼，黑泽明，等供图. 焦雄屏，译. 北京：北京联合出版公司，2008.

[10] 李道新. 中国电影文化史（1905—2004）[M]. 北京：北京大学出版社，2005.

[11] 李刚. 论中国第五代导演的文化精神 [M]. 北京：中国社会科学出版社，2008.

[12] 李少白. 中国电影史 [M]. 北京：高等教育出版社，2006.

[13] 陆绍阳. 视听语言 [M]. 3版. 北京：北京大学出版社，2021.

[14] 吕思勉. 中国文化常识 [M]. 北京：天地出版社，2019.

[15] 彭吉象. 影视美学 [M]. 3版. 北京：北京大学出版社，2019.

[16] 向达. 唐代长安与西域文明 [M]. 北京：商务印书馆，2015.

[17] 杨远婴. 电影理论读本 [M]. 修订版. 北京：北京联合出版公司，2017.

［18］张阿利，赵涛．中国西部电影精品读解［M］．北京：高等教育出版社，2021．

［19］张会军，陈浥，王鸿海．影片分析透视手册［M］．北京：中国电影出版社，2003．

［20］赵卫防．香港电影艺术史［M］．北京：文化艺术出版社，2017．

［21］朱文杰．吉祥陕西［M］．西安：太白文艺出版社，2015．